EVALUATION
RESEARCH

PRENTICE-HALL METHODS OF SOCIAL SCIENCE SERIES

EDITORS
Herbert Costner
Neil Smelser

CAROL H. WEISS
Columbia University

EVALUATION
RESEARCH

Methods for Assessing Program Effectiveness

PRENTICE-HALL, INC., Englewood Cliffs, New Jersey

ISBN: P 0-13-292193-6

Library of Congress Catalog Card Number: 71-179447
Printed in the United States of America

19   18   17   16   15

PRENTICE-HALL INTERNATIONAL, INC., *London*
PRENTICE-HALL OF AUSTRALIA, PTY. LTD., *Sydney*
PRENTICE-HALL OF CANADA, LTD., *Toronto*
PRENTICE-HALL OF INDIA PRIVATE LTD., *New Delhi*
PRENTICE-HALL OF JAPAN, INC., *Tokyo*

TO MY HUSBAND
who doesn't talk much about women's liberation
but has always practiced it

Preface

This book deals with the application of research methods to the evaluation of social programs—programs in education, social work, corrections, health, mental health, job training, technical assistance, community action, law, and so on. It is designed for use as a basic text in courses on evaluation research in the growing number of schools that offer such a course, and as a supplementary text in the large number of courses on research methods. It is written at a level appropriate for undergraduate as well as graduate instruction, with clear explanation of concepts and techniques and considerable illustrative material.

The basic theme of the book is that evaluation uses the methods and tools of social research but applies them in an action context that is intrinsically inhospitable to them. Researchers who embark on evaluation with training only in traditional research methods often bog down in the complexities of the action setting. A principal aim of the book is to acquaint the reader with the realities of evaluation life. We even considered the titles "Life Among the Evaluators" and "Inside Evaluation Research" as a way of indicating our concern with the real-life issues in evaluation. We assume that the reader has an acquaintance with basic research methods; even a nodding acquaintance will get him through the book. Other volumes in the Methods of Social Science Series give greater detail on topics such as data analysis that we skim by lightly. Our emphasis is on applying research methods in the environment of an action program. We intend to alert readers to prevalent issues and problems and offer guidance for adapting textbook methods to suit the special world that the evaluator inhabits.

There are enormous demands today for skilled evaluators in all the new federal programs in education, vocational education, rehabilitation, crime and delinquency, mental health, antipoverty, health, community planning, model cities, family planning, addiction services, and so on. There is a need, too, for greater understanding of evaluation purposes and processes by practitioners and administrators in these fields who are expected (and often legally required) to cooperate with evaluation efforts and to put to use the findings that emerge from study. The book should be valuable to students and professionals with both functions—to those who engage in evaluation research and those who are involved in policy-making, administration, and conduct of programs that are evaluated. Our aim is to help the reader conceptualize and understand evaluation research as well as to offer advice on how to do it.

With the great necessity for more effective programs to meet the social needs confronting the nation, evaluation research is increasingly important as a source of knowledge and direction. It tells which programs work and which do not, and points the way to better formulation of policy and program. It can be even more helpful as it proceeds to identify the effects of specific strategies and components *within* programs and separates out those that contribute to favorable outcomes from those that are ineffective or counterproductive. Under appropriate conditions, it can also contribute to the development of basic knowledge. Evaluation investigates the consequences of dynamic programs that attempt to alter key variables in people's lives. Finding out how successful these efforts have been, and why, can lead to discoveries about basic concepts of human behavior and social structure—if the research is carried out with care and insight.

Evaluation has not yet realized its full promise as a guide for improving the rationality of social policy. Its potential is unquestioned; its current state is less impressive. Evaluation demands an imposing array of talents, not only technical research skills but also political, social, and relational skills that pave the way for the evaluator to apply his expertise. The book thus goes beyond the usual bounds of a "methods" book to discuss ways by which the evaluator can help institute the conditions that permit sound research. By focusing on the structures within which evaluation takes place, as well as methods and techniques suited to the evaluative task, we hope to make a modest contribution to improving the state of evaluation practice.

Many people have helped to provide the experience that went into this book. I would like to thank the funders, program directors, practitioners, and research colleagues with whom I collaborated and consulted on over a dozen evaluation studies, and the program participants who cooperated in the evaluations. I learned a great deal as evaluation consultant to the Office of Juvenile Delinquency and Youth Development of the Department of Health, Education, and Welfare, and the Model Cities Administration of the Department of Housing and Urban Development. Similarly informative was the opportunity to analyze the evaluation experience of projects supported by the National Institute of Mental Health. I have profited from the ideas of Herbert Hyman, Edward Suchman, Peter Rossi, and Howard Freeman. In the preparation of the manuscript, I owe much to the comments of Donald Campbell, Northwestern University, on research design; Howard Davis of the National Institute of Mental Health on the utilization of evaluation research; Clarence Teng, New York City Rand Institute, on cost-benefit analysis; Allen Schick of the Brookings Institution on program-planning-budgeting; but none of them is responsible for my interpretation of the good advice they gave. Karen Louis was both diligent and selective in helping to compile the bibliography. I would particularly like to thank Herbert Costner for his careful review of the manuscript and Allen Barton for the continuing benefit of his critical judgment.

CAROL H. WEISS

Contents

x

3

4

5

6

EVALUATION
RESEARCH

1

Introduction

Evaluation is an elastic word that stretches to cover judgments of many kinds. People talk about evaluation of a worker's job performance, evaluation of a movie script, evaluation of the sales potential of a new detergent. What all the uses of the word have in common is the notion of judging merit. Someone is examining and weighing a phenomenon (a person, a thing, an idea) against some explicit or implicit yardstick.

In this book we will be talking about evaluation of one particular kind of phenomenon: social programs designed to improve the lot of people. The programs are diverse; they can deal with education, social welfare, health, housing, mental health, legal services, corrections, economic development, and many other fields. They can be aimed to change people's knowledge, attitudes, values, behaviors, the institutions with which they deal, or the communities in which they live. Their common characteristic is the goal of making life better and more rewarding for the people they serve.

Furthermore, we are concerned here with a specific method of evaluation—evaluation research. The tools of research are pressed into service to make the judging process more accurate and objective. In its research guise, evaluation establishes clear and specific criteria for success. It collects evidence systematically from a representative sample of the units of concern. It usually translates the evidence into quantitative terms (23 percent of the audience, grades of 85 or better), and compares it with the criteria that were set. It then draws conclusions about the effectiveness, the merit, the success, of the phenomenon under study.

The research process takes more time and costs more money than off-hand evaluations that rely on intuition, opinion, or trained sensibility, but it provides a rigor that is particularly important when (1) the outcomes to be evaluated are complex, hard to observe, made up of many elements reacting in diverse ways; (2) the decisions that will follow are important and expensive; and (3) evidence is needed to convince other people about the validity of the conclusions.

In the past decade social programs at all levels have expanded enormously. Some are logical extensions of earlier efforts, some represent radical departures from the past and a plunge into uncharted waters. Decision makers want (and need) to know: How well is the program meeting the purposes for which it was established? Should it be continued, expanded, cut back, changed, or abandoned? The answers are hard to come by through informal means. The best informed people (the staff running the program) tend toward optimism and in any case have a stake in reporting success. Many programs provide a variety of services and deal with large numbers of participants. A handful of "consumer testimonials" or a quick tour of inspection can hardly gauge their effectiveness. Decisions about future operations will affect the fate of many people and involve sizable sums of money, and the decision makers are often people (legislators, boards of directors) sufficiently removed from the program to want hard facts on which to base their decisions. Under these conditions, evaluation research appears well suited to the task of producing the requisite information, and in recent years it has become a growth enterprise.

Contributions to Rational
Decision Making

Evaluation research is viewed by its partisans as a way to increase the rationality of policy making. With objective information on the outcomes of programs, wise decisions can be made on budget allocations and program planning. Programs that yield good results will be expanded; those that make poor showings will be abandoned or drastically modified. The following excerpt from Congresswoman Dwyer's (Republican, New Jersey) *Report to the People*, although it does not mention evaluation research, captures the rationale of the case for evaluation:

It is becoming increasingly clear that much of our investment in such areas as education, health, poverty, jobs, housing, urban development, transportation and the like is not returning adequate dividends in terms of results. Without for a moment lessening our commitment to provide for these pressing human needs, one of Congress' major, though oft-delayed, challenges must be to reassess our multitude of social programs, concentrate (indeed, expand) resources on programs that *work* where the needs are greatest, and reduce or eliminate the remainder. We no longer have the time nor the money to fritter away on non-essentials which won't produce the needed visible impact on problems.[1]

Both on the national and the local scale, the application of social science knowledge and methodology is expected to have beneficial effects: improve decision making, lead to the planning of better programs, and so serve program participants in more relevant, more beneficial, and more efficient ways. The production of objective evidence is seen as a way to reduce the politicking, the self-serving maneuvers, and the log-rolling that commonly attend decision making at every level from the Congress to the local school. Data will replace favors and other political negotiations, so that the most rational decisions will be reached.

In these terms, the history of evaluation research to date has been disappointing. Few examples can be cited of important contributions to policy and program. Part of the reason lies in the remarkable resistance of organizations to unwanted information—and unwanted change. Even evidence of outright failure can leave some institutions figuratively and literally unmoved. Part of the fault lies in the way evaluation itself is structured, staffed, and operated. There are fissures between the intended purposes of evaluation and the kinds of studies conducted. That indeed is the subject of much of this book.

But part of the disillusionment with the contributions of evaluation derives from the unrealistic nature of the expectations. An evaluation study does not generally come up with final and unequivocal findings about the worth of a program. Its results often show small, ambiguous changes, minor effects, outcomes influenced by the specific events of the place and the moment. It may require continued study over time and across projects to speak with confidence about success and failure.

Furthermore, for decision makers, evaluation evidence of outcome is only one input out of many. They must consider a host of other factors, from public receptivity and participant reaction, to costs, availability of

[1] Rep. Florence P. Dwyer, *Report to the People,* 12th District New Jersey, XIV, No. 1, January 22, 1970.

staff and facilities, and possible alternatives. Those who look to evaluation to take the politics out of decision making are bound to be disappointed. Within every organization, decisions are reached through negotiation and accommodation, through politics. This is the system we have for attaching *value* to facts. Different actors bring different values and priorities to the decision-making process. Evaluative facts have an impact on collective decisions only to the extent that program effectiveness is perceived as valuable. And program effectiveness—inevitably and justifiably—competes for influence on decisions with considerations of acceptability, feasibility, and ideology. Sometimes it is emotionally and politically rewarding to run a program even when it has been shown to have little effect if the alternative is to do nothing for a particular group. Sometimes the existing ideological climate precludes the adoption of more effective programs if these violate cherished assumptions and values.

It is within this context that evaluation should be viewed. What evaluation *can* do is provide data that reduce uncertainties and clarify the gains and losses that different decisions incur. In this way, it allows decision makers to apply their values and preferences more accurately, with better knowledge of the trade-offs that alternative decisions involve.

Purpose of Evaluation Research

The purpose of evaluation research is to measure the effects of a program against the goals it set out to accomplish as a means of contributing to subsequent decision making about the program and improving future programming. Within that definition are four key features: "To measure the effects" refers to the *research methodology* that is used. "The effects" emphasizes the *outcomes* of the program, rather than its efficiency, honesty, morale, or adherence to rules or standards. The comparison of effects with goals stresses the use of explicit *criteria* for judging how well the program is doing. The contribution to subsequent decision making and the improvement of future programming denote the *social purpose* of evaluation.

Programs are of many kinds. Not only do they range over a gamut of fields; they also vary in scope, size, duration, clarity and specificity of program input, complexity of goals, and innovativeness. These differences in programs have important consequences for the type of evaluation that is feasible and productive. It is one thing to evaluate the effects of a small, short-term, specific, well-defined program, such as a training film. It is a far different and more difficult matter to evaluate the effects of the national antipoverty program, with its diversity of methods, actions, and goals. The evaluator may find it rewarding to become aware of some of the differences among programs so that he can think about ways to shape evaluative approaches and method to suit.

Scope. The program being evaluated may cover the nation, a region, state, city, neighborhood, or be limited to one specific site (a classroom). Some programs turn up in scattered locations (a methadone treatment program for drug addicts in ten hospitals around the country).

Size. Programs can serve a few people or reach thousands or even millions.

Duration. A program can last a few hours, days, or weeks, a specified number of months or years, or go on indefinitely (the Boy Scout program, public school education).

Clarity and specificity of program input. What it is that the program actually *does* may be well-defined and precise; for example, brighter street lights may be installed on given streets in an attempt to reduce crime. Many programs have some degree of clarity (a new science curriculum, foster home placement), since a particular method or specific materials are being employed, but different staff members may vary in style and skill in administering them. At the extreme there are programs that are diffuse, highly variable, and difficult even to describe (a program of interagency planning).

Complexity and time span of goals. Some programs are intended to produce a clear-cut change or changes (improvement in reading skills, placement in a job). Others seek more complex goals (make children better citizens, improve mental health, improve family functioning) that are harder to define and measure. A goal such as "improving the quality of urban life" contains within it not only a large number of subgoals (that must be made explicit) but also ambiguous subgoals (improving the esthetics of the urban scene) that pose awesome problems of conceptualization and measurement.

Another issue is the time span of the goals. It is easier for the evaluator to deal with intended changes that manifest themselves quickly than with those that become evident or sure only after half a lifetime.

Innovativeness. At one end of the continuum are programs that mark a drastic shift from accustomed methods of operation. At the other are regular ongoing programs of established agencies.

The characteristics of the program will affect the kind of evaluation that can be done and the purposes that evaluation can serve. In Chapter 2 we will examine the subject of purpose in greater detail. One of the problems in doing good evaluation research is that different people see different purposes for the evaluation and want to use its results in different ways. Unless and until the evaluator finds out specifically who wants to know what, with what end in view, the evaluation study is likely to be mired in a morass of conflicting expectations.

Comparison Between Evaluation and Other Research

Evaluation applies the methods of social research. Principles and methods that apply to all other types of research apply here as well. Everything we know about design, measurement, and analysis comes into play in planning and conducting an evaluation study. What distinguishes evaluation research is not method or subject matter, but intent—the purpose for which it is done.

Differences

Use for decision making. Evaluation is intended for use. Where basic research puts the emphasis on the production of knowledge and leaves its use to the natural processes of dissemination and application, evaluation starts out with *use* in mind. In its ideal form, evaluation is conducted for a client who has decisions to make and who looks to the evaluation for answers on which to base his decisions. Use is often less direct and immediate than that, but it always provides the rationale for evaluation.

Program-derived questions. The questions that evaluation considers are the decision maker's questions rather than the evaluator's. Unlike the basic researcher who formulates his own hypotheses, the evaluator deals in the currency of program concerns. He has a good deal of say about the shape of the study, and he approaches it from the perspectives of his own knowledge and discipline. He is usually free to embroider it with investigations of particular concern to him. But the core of the study represents matters of administrative and programmatic interest. The common evaluation hypothesis is that the program is accomplishing what it set out to do.

Judgmental quality. Evaluation compares "what is" with "what should be." Although the investigator himself remains unbiased and objective, he is concerned with phenomena that demonstrate whether the program is achieving its intended goals. However the questions for study are formulated, somewhere in the formulation appears a concern with measuring up to stated criteria. This element of judgment against criteria is basic to evaluation and differentiates it from other kinds of research. The statement of program goals by the staff of the program is therefore essential to evaluation. It comes as a particular blow to discover that programs do not generally have clear statements of goals. In Chapter 3 we will explore the problems involved.

Action setting. Evaluation takes place in an action setting, where the most important thing that is going on is the program. The program is serving people. If there are conflicts in requirements between program and evaluation, priority is likely to go to program. Program staff often control access to the people served in the program. They may control access to records and files. They are in charge of assignment of participants to program activities and locations. Not infrequently, research requirements (for "before" data, for control groups) run up against established program procedures, which tend to prevail.

Role conflicts. Interpersonal frictions are not uncommon between evaluators and practitioners. The practitioners' roles and the norms of their service professions tend to make them unresponsive to research requests and promises. As they see it, the imperative is service; evaluation research is not likely to make such contributions to the improvement of program service that it is worth disruptions and delays. Often, they believe strongly in the worth of the program they are providing, and see little need for evaluation at all. Furthermore, the judgmental quality of evaluation research means that the merit of their activities is being weighed. In a sense, as they see it, they are on trial. If the results of evaluation are negative, if it is found that the program is not accomplishing the purposes for which it was established, then the program—and possibly their jobs—are in jeopardy. The possibilities for friction are obvious.

Publication. Basic research is published. Its dissemination to the research and professional fraternity is essential and unquestioned. In evaluation, probably the majority of study reports go unpublished. Program administrators and staff often believe that the information was generated to answer their questions, and they are not eager to have their linen washed in public. Evaluators are sometimes so pressed for time, or so discouraged about the compromises they have made in research design, that they submit a mimeographed report to the agency and go on to the next study. Yet if progress is to be made in learning which types of programs work and which do not, a cumulative information base is essential. Only through publication will results build up. Even when results show that the program has had little effect, it is important that others learn of the findings so that ineffective programs are not duplicated again and again.

Of course, not all evaluation studies are worth publication. Poorly conducted studies are more misleading than useful. Further, if the evaluator has addressed the issues in such concrete and specific terms that his results are not generalizable beyond the immediate program, there is little to report to others. Hovland makes a distinction between "program testing" and "variable testing." If only the specific program has been tested and not the concepts or the approaches (variables) on which it is based, the study makes little contribution to developing knowledge.

Allegiance. The evaluation researcher has a dual, perhaps a triple, allegiance. He has obligations to the organization that funds his study. He owes it a report of unqualified objectivity and as much usefulness for action as he can devise. Beyond the specific organization, he has responsibilities to contribute to the improvement of social change efforts. Whether or not the organization supports the study's conclusions, the evaluator often perceives an obligation to work for their application for the sake of the common weal. On both counts, he has commitments in the action arena. He also has an obligation to the development of knowledge and to his profession. As a social scientist, he seeks to advance the frontiers of knowledge about how intervention affects human lives and institutions.

If some of the differences between evaluation research and more academic social research have made the lot of the evaluator look unduly harsh, there are compensations. One of the most rewarding is the opportunity to participate actively in the meeting of scientific knowledge and social action and to contribute to the improvement of societal programs. It is this opportunity that has attracted so many able researchers to the field of evaluation research despite the disabilities that attend its practice.

Similarities

There are important similarities, too, between evaluation and other brands of research. Like other research, evaluation attempts to describe, to understand the relationships between variables, and to trace out the causal sequence. Because it is studying a program that intervenes in people's lives with the intention of causing change, evaluation can often make direct inferences about the causal links that lead from program to effect.

Evaluators use the whole gamut of research methods to collect information—interviews, questionnaires, tests of knowledge and skill, attitude inventories, observation, content analysis of documents, records, examination of physical evidence. Ingenious evaluators can find fitting ways of exploring a wide range of effects. The kind of data-collection scheme to be used depends on the type of information needed to answer the specific questions that the evaluation poses.

The classic design for evaluations has been the experimental model. This involves measurement of the relevant variables for at least two equivalent groups—one that has been exposed to the program and one that has not. But many other designs are used in evaluation research—case studies, post-program surveys, time series, correlational studies, and so on. The experimental model that has long reigned as the ideal (if often neglected) design for evaluation research has recently been challenged on several grounds. We will discuss these issues further in Chapter 4.

There is no cut-and-dried formula to offer evaluators for the "best" or most suitable way of pursuing their study. Much depends on the uses to be made of the study, the decisions pending, and the information needs of decision makers. Much also depends (unfortunately) on the constraints in the program setting—the limits placed on the study by the realities of time, place, and people. Money is an issue, too. Textbooks rarely mention the grubby matter of funding, but limited funds impose inevitable restrictions on how much can be studied over how long a period. Thus evaluation methods often represent a compromise between the ideal and the feasible.

Evaluation is sometimes regarded as a lower order of research, particularly in academic circles, than "basic" or "pure" research. Evaluators are looked down on as the drones of the research fraternity, technicians drudging away on dull issues and compromising their integrity out in the corrupt world. But as any working evaluator will heartfeelingly tell you, evaluation calls for a higher level of skills than research that is under the researcher's complete control. It is relatively easy to run experiments in an insulated laboratory with captive subjects. But to make research work when it is coping with the complexities of real people in real programs run by real organizations takes skill—and some guts. The evaluator has to know a good deal about the formulation of the research question, study design, sampling, measurement, analysis, and interpretation. He has to know what is in the research methodology texts, and then he has to learn how to apply that knowledge in a setting that is often inhospitable to important features of his knowledge. If he persists in his textbook stance, he runs the risk of doing work irrelevant to the needs of the agency, antagonizing the program personnel with whom he works, and seeing his study results go unused— if indeed the work is ever completed. So he sometimes has to find alternative ways of conducting his study, while at the same time he stands ready to defend to the death those elements of the study that cannot be compromised.

2

Purposes of Evaluation

In this chapter, we will discuss the purposes, acknowledged and unacknowledged, for which people decide to undertake program evaluation. We suggest that the evaluator find out what decision makers really seek from the study and how they expect to use the results. With this knowledge, he can most effectively tailor the study to provide information for decision making. The location of the evaluation unit—where it fits into the organizational structure—can make a difference in whether the study has sufficient latitude to be useful.

Before we get on with these matters, let us raise a prior question. Is evaluation always warranted? Should all programs if they are good little programs go out and get themselves evaluated? The answer, heretical as it may seem, is No. Evaluation as an applied research is committed to the principle of utility. If it is not going to have any effect on decisions, it is an exercise in futility. Evaluation is probably not worth doing in four kinds of circumstances:

1. When there are no questions about the program. It goes on, and decisions about its future either do not come up or have already been made.

2. When the program has no clear orientation. Program staff improvise activities from day to day, based on little thought and less principle, and the program shifts and changes, wanders around and seeks direction. There is little here to call "a program."

3. When people who should know cannot agree on what the program is trying to achieve. If there are vast discrepancies in perceived goals, evaluation has no ground to stand on.

4. When there is not enough money or no staff sufficiently qualified to conduct the evalution. Evaluation is a demanding business, calling for time, money, imagination, tenacity, and skill.

There are those who argue that even in such dismal circumstances, evaluation research can produce something of value, some glimmering of insight that will light a candle for the future. This is a fetching notion, and from time to time in this volume, we succumb to it. But experience suggests that even good evaluation studies of well-defined programs, directed to clear decisional purposes, often wind up as litter in the bureaucratic mill. It will be a rare study indeed that provides illumination under unfavorable conditions.

Overt and Covert Purposes

People decide to have a program evaluated for many different reasons, from the eminently rational to the patently political. Ideally, an administrator is seeking answers to pressing questions about the program's future: Should it be continued? Should it be expanded? Should changes be made in its operation? But there are occasions when he turns to evaluation for less legitimate reasons.

Postponement. The decision maker may be looking for ways to delay a decision. Instead of resorting to the usual ploy of appointing a committee and waiting for its report, he can commission an evaluation study, which takes even longer.

Ducking responsibility. Sometimes one faction in the program organization is espousing one course of action and another faction is opposing it. The administrators look to evaluation to get them off the hook by producing dispassionate evidence that will make the decision for them. There are cases in which administrators know what the decision will be even before they call in the evaluators, but want to cloak it in the legitimate trappings of research.

Public relations. Occasionally, evaluation is seen as a way of self-glorification. The administrator believes that he has a highly successful program and looks for a way to make it visible. A good study will fill the bill. Copies of the report, favorable of course, can be sent to boards of trustees, members of legislative committees, executives of philanthropic foundations who give large sums to successful programs, and other influential people. Suchman [1] suggests two related purposes: eyewash and whitewash. In an eyewash evaluation, an attempt is made to justify a weak program by selecting for evaluation only those aspects that look good on the surface. A whitewash attempts to cover up program failure by avoiding any objective appraisal.

The program administrator's motives are not, of course, necessarily crooked or selfish. Often, there is a need to justify the program to the people who pay the bills, and he is seeking support for a concept and a project in which he believes. Generating support for existing programs is a common motive for embarking on evaluation.

Fulfilling grant requirements. Increasingly, the decision to evaluate stems from sources outside the program. Many federal grants for demonstration projects and innovative programs are tagged with an evaluation requirement; for example, all projects for disadvantaged pupils funded under Title I of the Elementary and Secondary Education Act are required to be evaluated.

From the point of view of the funders, who are taking a chance on an untried project, it is reasonable to require that there be some evidence on the extent to which the project is working. To the operators of a project, the demands of starting up and running the new program take priority. Plagued as they often are by immediate problems of staffing, budgets, logistics, community relations, and all the other trials of pioneers, they tend to neglect the evaluation. They see it mainly as a ritual designed to placate the funding bodies, without any real usefulness to them.

Evaluation, then, is a rational enterprise often undertaken for nonrational, or at least noninformational, reasons. We could continue the catalog of the varieties of covert purposes (justifying a program to Congress, "getting" the program director, increasing the prestige of the agency), but the important point is that such motives have consequences for the evaluation that can be serious and bleak.[2]

[1] Edward A. Suchman, "Action for What? A Critique of Evaluative Research," in *The Organization, Management, and Tactics of Social Research,* ed. Richard O'Toole (Cambridge, Mass.: Schenkman Publishing Co., Inc., 1970).

[2] See Sar Levitan, "Facts, Fancies, and Freeloaders in Evaluating Antipoverty Programs," *Poverty and Human Resources Abstracts,* IV, No. 6 (1969), 13–16; Richard H. Hall, "The Applied Sociologist and Organizational Sociology," in *So-*

An evaluator who is asked to study a particular program usually assumes that he is there because people want answers about what the program is doing well and poorly. When this is not the case, he may in his naïveté become a pawn in intraorganizational power struggles, a means of delaying action, or the rallying point for one ideology or another. Some evaluators have found only after their study was done that they had unwittingly played a role in a larger political game. They found that nobody was particularly interested in applying their results to the decisions at hand, but only in using them (or any quotable piece of them) as ammunition to destroy or to justify.

Lesson No. 1 for the evaluator newly arrived on the scene is: Find out who initiated the idea of having an evaluation of the program and for what purposes. Were there other groups in the organization who questioned or objected to the evaluation? What were their motives? Is there real commitment among practitioners, administrators, and/or funders to using the results of the evaluation to improve future decision making? If the real purposes for the evaluation are not oriented to better decision making and there is little commitment to applying results, the project is probably a poor candidate for evaluation. The evaluator might well ponder whether he wishes to get involved in the situation or whether he can find more productive uses for his talents elsewhere.

Intended Uses

Even when evaluation is undertaken for bona fide purposes (that is, to learn how well the program is reaching its goals), people can have widely differing expectations of the kinds of answers that will be produced. If the evaluator is not to be caught unawares, it behooves him to know from the outset what kinds of answers are expected from his study.[3]

---

ciology in Action, ed. Arthur B. Shostak (Homewood, Ill.: Dorsey Press, Inc., 1966), pp. 33–38; Joseph W. Eaton, "Symbolic and Substantive Evaluative Research," *Administrative Science Quarterly,* VI, No. 4 (1962), 421–42; Lewis A. Dexter, "Impressions About Utility and Wastefulness in Applied Social Science Studies," *American Behavioral Scientist,* IX, No. 6 (1966), 9–10.

[3] Downs makes the point that the extent of applied research should be economically justified by the value of the information it produces for decision making. Evaluators, like other researchers, can become fascinated with the problem and do more research than the program needs. But he also stresses the point that clients frequently need redefinition of the problem and the suggestion of alternative approaches. Anthony Downs, "Some Thoughts on Giving People Economic Advice," *American Behavioral Scientist,* IX, No. 1 (1965), 30–32. Of course, far more common than spending too much money is trying to conduct evaluation with funds grossly inadequate for the extent and precision of the results expected.

Who expects what?

Expectations for the evaluation generally vary with a person's position in the system.[4] Top policy makers need the kind of information that will help them address the broad issues: Should the program be continued or dropped, institutionalized throughout the system or limited to a pilot program, continued with the same procedures and techniques or modified? Should more money be allocated to this program or to others? They want information on the overall effectiveness of the program.

The directors of the program face other issues. They want to know not only how well their program is achieving the desired ends, but also which general strategies are more or less successful, which are achieving results most efficiently and economically, which features of the program are essential and which can be changed or dropped.

Direct-service staff deal with individuals and small groups. They have practical day-to-day concerns about techniques. Should they spend more time on developing good work habits and less time on teaching subject matter? Put more emphasis on group discussions or films or lectures? Should they accept more younger people (who are not already set in their ways) or more older people (who have greater responsibilities and more need)? Practitioners, who are accustomed to relying on their own experience and intuitive judgment, often challenge evaluation to come up with something practical on topics such as these.

Nor do these three sets of actors—policy makers, program directors, and practitioners—exhaust the list of those with a possible oar in the evaluation. The funders of evaluation research, particularly when they are outside the direct line of operations, may have an interest in adding to the pool of knowledge in the field. They may want answers less to operating questions than to questions of theory and method. Can social group work help improve the parental performance of young couples? Does increasing the available career opportunities for low-income youth result in less juvenile deliquency? If coordination among community health services is increased, will people receive better health care? Here is another purpose for evaluation—to test propositions about the utility of concepts or models of service. The public too has a stake, as taxpayers, as parents of schoolchildren, as contributors to voluntary organizations.[5] They are concerned that their money is wisely and efficiently spent.

[4] A useful discussion appears in Louis Ferman, "Some Perspectives on Evaluating Social Welfare Programs," *Annals of the American Academy of Political and Social Science*, Vol. 385 (September 1969), 143–56.

[5] Edward Wynne, in "Evaluating Educational Programs: A Symposium," *Urban Review*, III, No. 4 (1969), 19–20.

Recently, another actor has entered the decision-making arena—the consumer of services. He may see a use for evaluation in asking "client-eye" questions about the program under study. Is the program serving the goals that the intended beneficiaries of service value? [6] Recently, there has been rising opposition, particularly in some black communities, to traditional formulations of program goals.[7] Activists are concerned not only with how well programs work to improve school achievement or health care, but also with their political legitimacy. They are interested in community participation or community control of programs and institutions. When such issues are paramount, evaluative questions derive from a radically different perspective.

Compatibility of purposes

With all the possible uses for evaluation to serve, the evaluator has to make choices. The all-purpose evaluation is a myth. Although a number of different types of questions can be considered within the bounds of a single study, this takes meticulous planning and design. Inevitably not even the best-planned study will provide information on all the questions that people will think of. In fact, some purposes for evaluation are incompatible with others. Let us consider the evaluation of a particular educational program for slow learners.

The teaching staff wants to use the results to improve the presentations and teaching methods of the course, session by session, in order to maximize student learning. The state college of education wants to know whether the instructional program, based on a particular theory of learning, will improve pupil performance. In the first case, the evaluator will have to examine immediate short-term effects (learnings after the morning drill). He need not be concerned about generalizing the results to other populations, and needs neither control groups nor sophisticated statistics. He will want to maximize feedback of results to the teachers so that they can modify their techniques as they go along.

On the other hand, when evaluation is testing the proposition that a program developed from certain theories of learning will be successful with slow learners, it is concerned with long-range effects. It requires rigorous design so that observed results can be attributed to the stimulus of the

---

[6] Philip H. Taylor, "The Role and Function of Educational Research," *Educational Research*, IX, No. 1 (1966), 11–15; Edmund deS. Brunner, "Evaluation Research in Adult Education," *International Review of Community Development*, No. 17–18 (1967), 97–102.

[7] David K. Cohen, "Politics and Research: Evaluation of Social Action Programs in Education," *Review of Educational Research*, XL, No. 2 (1970), 232.

program and not to extraneous events. The results have to be generalizable beyond the specific group of students. The instructional program should be insulated from alterations during its course in order to preserve the clarity of the program that led to the effects observed.

In theory, it is possible to achieve both an assessment of overall program effectiveness and a test of the effectiveness of component strategies. Textbooks on the design of experiments [8] present methods of factorial design that allow the experimenter to discover both total effect and the effects of each "experimental treatment." In practice, evaluation can seldom go about the business so systematically. The constraints of the field situation hobble the evalution—too few clients, demand for quick feedback of information, inadequate funds, "contamination" of the special-treatment groups by receipt of other services, drop-outs from the program, lack of access to records and data, changes in program, and so on.

Some researchers say that to try to satisfy a multiplicity of demands and uses under usual field conditions invites frustration. The evaluator who identifies the key decision pending and gears his study to supplying information relevant to that issue is on firmer ground. Others believe that there are ways—not necessarily formal and elegant—to study a range of issues concurrently.[9] Some of these methods will be discussed in Chapters 3 and 4. Nevertheless, it remains important for the evaluator to know the priority among the purposes. If the crunch comes, he can jettison the extra baggage and fight for the essentials.

Formative and summative evaluation

We have identified several types of uses for evaluation. Evaluation can be asked to investigate the extent of program success so that decisions such as these can be made:

1. To continue or discontinue the program
2. To improve its practices and procedures
3. To add or drop specific program strategies and techniques
4. To institute similar programs elsewhere

[8] A good example is B. J. Winer, *Statistical Principles in Experimental Design* (New York: McGraw-Hill Book Company, 1962). F. Stuart Chapin, W. G. Cochran and G. M. Cox, D. R. Cox, A. L. Edwards, R. A. Fisher, R. E. Kirk and E. F. Lindquist, among others, have also written useful texts on experimental design. Some of these are listed in the third section of the bibliography.

[9] See Robert E. Stake, "Generalizability of Program Evaluation: The Need for Limits," and James L. Wardrop, "Generalizability of Program Evaluation: The Dangers of Limits," *Educational Product Report,* II, No. 5 (1969), 38–40, 41–42.

5. To allocate resources among competing programs
6. To accept or reject a program approach or theory

A useful distinction has been introduced into the discussion of purpose by Scriven.[10] In discussing the evaluation of educational curriculums, he distinguishes between *formative* and *summative* evaluation. Formative evaluation produces information that is fed back during the development of a curriculum to help improve it. It serves the needs of developers. Summative evaluation is done after the curriculum is finished. It provides information about effectiveness to school decision makers who are considering adopting it.[11]

This distinction can be applied to other types of programs as well, with obvious advantages for the clarification of purpose. Many programs, however, are never "finished" in the sense that a curriculum is finished, and continued modification and adaptation will be necessary both at the original site and in other locations that use the program. The evaluator still has some hard thinking to do.

In practice, evaluation is most often called on to help with decisions about improving programs. Go/no-go, live-or-die decisions are relatively rare. Even when evaluation results show the program to be a failure, the usual reaction is to patch it up and try again. Rare, too, is the use of evaluation in theory-oriented tests of program approaches and models. These are more readily studied under controlled laboratory conditions. It is the search for improvements in strategies and techniques that supports much evaluation activity at present.

Even when decision makers start out with global questions (Is the program worth continuing?), they often end up receiving qualified results ("There are these good effects, but . . .") that lead them to look for ways to modify present practice. They become interested in the likelihood of improved results with different components, a different mix of services, different client groups, different staffing patterns, different organizational structure, different procedures and mechanics. One of the ironies of evaluation practice is that it has performed well at assessment of overall impact, suited to the uncommon go/no-go decision; it is relatively undeveloped in designs that produce information on the effectiveness of comparative strategies. We shall return to this point in Chapter 4.

[10] Michael Scriven, "The Methodology of Evaluation," in *Perspectives of Curriculum Evaluation,* ed. Ralph W. Tyler, Robert M. Gagné, and Michael Scriven, AERA Monograph Series on Curriculum Evaluation, No. 1 (Chicago: Rand McNally & Co., 1967), pp. 39–83.

[11] See also Thomas J. Hastings, "Curriculum Evaluation: The Why of Outcomes," *Journal of Educational Measurement,* III, No. 3 (1966), 27–32.

Whose Use Shall Be Served?

Some possible users of the evaluation have been mentioned:

1. A funding organization (government, private, foundation)
2. A national agency (governmental, private)
3. A local agency
4. The directors of the specific project
5. Direct-service staff
6. Clients of the program
7. Scholars in the disciplines and professions

Which purposes shall the evaluation serve and for whom? In some cases, the question is academic. The evaluator is on the staff of some organization—national organization, pilot program—and he does the job assigned to him. But more often, the evaluator has a number of options open. If he is on the staff of an outside research organization that is being asked to undertake the evaluation, he may have the opportunity to negotiate the purpose and focus of the study. Even if he is more closely attached to the project, there is commonly such an amazing lack of clarity among the other parties that he has wide room to maneuver.

If he can help shape the basic focus of the study, the evaluator will consider a number of things. First is probably his own set of values. A summer program for ghetto youth can be evaluated for city officialdom to see if it cools out the kids and prevents riots and looting. The evaluator may want to view the program from the youths' perspective as well and see if it has improved their job prospects, work skills, and enjoyment. The data such a study produces can give a wider frame of reference to the decision of whether or not to continue the summer programs. It is important that the evaluator be able to live with the study, its uses, and his conscience at the same time.

Beyond this point, the paramount consideration in what use the study should be designed to serve is: What decision has to be made? The pending question may be one of extending a small pilot program in one hospital ward to other wards in the same hospital. It may be allocating money to one project or to another. There may have to be a decision on the adoption of one technique (reduced case loads, nonprofessional aides) throughout the system. Perhaps the upcoming decisions have to do with staffing, structure, or target populations. Once the evaluator finds out what key decisions are pending and when they will come up, he can gear his study to provide the maximum payoff.

Often there is no critical decision pending, at least that anyone can identify at the moment. There are, however, "users" who are interested in learning from the study and applying the results and others who are not. When the local program managers are conscientiously seeking better ways to serve their clients while the policy makers at higher levels are looking primarily for "program vindicators," the local managers' questions may deserve more attention. On the other hand, if the locals want a whitewash and the higher levels want to know where to put further appropriations, the evaluator should place more emphasis on comparative assessment of overall outcome.

The next task, then, is designing the evaluation to provide the answers that are needed. Finding out what answers are needed is not always an easy job. As we shall see in Chapter 3, it is the rare program that is articulate about goals, objectives, criteria, and bases for decision. Nevertheless, based on his best estimate of intended use, the evaluator has to make decisions on the measures to be used (see Chapter 3), sources of information (Chapter 3), and research design (Chapter 4). He will be abetted or hindered by the location of the evaluation within the organizational structure. It is to this issue that we now turn.

Structure of the Evaluation

An evaluation study can be staffed and structured in different ways. A research unit or department within the program agency can do the evaluation, or special evaluators can be hired and attached to the program. (This is often the way federally funded demonstration projects handle their evaluation requirement.) Outsiders, usually university faculty members, are sometimes paid to serve as consultants, and either advise the evaluators on staff or carry out some of the evaluation tasks themselves in close cooperation with staff. These kinds of arrangements can be lumped together as "in-house."

Another approach is for the agency to contract with an outside research organization to do the study. The research organization, whether it is an academic group, a nonprofit organization, or a commercial firm, is responsible to the persons (and the level in the program agency) who commission it. Still another kind of arrangement is for a national agency (such as the U.S. Office of Education or the national YMCA) to employ a research organization to study a number of the local programs it supports or oversees.

Inside vs. outside evaluation

There is a long tradition of controversy, mainly oral, about whether in-house or outside evaluations are preferable.[12] The answer seems to be that neither has a monopoly on the advantages. Some of the factors to be considered are administrative confidence, objectivity, understanding of the program, potential for utilization, and autonomy.

Administrative confidence. Administrators must have confidence in the professional skills of the evaluation staff. Sometimes agency personnel are impressed only by the credentials and reputations of academic researchers and assume that the research people it has on staff or can hire are second-raters. Conversely, it may view outside evaluators as too remote from the realities, too ivory-tower and abstract, to produce information of practical value. Occasionally, it is important to ensure public confidence by engaging evaluators who have no stake in the program to be studied. Competence, of course, is a big factor in ensuring confidence and deserves priority consideration.

Objectivity. Objectivity requires that evaluators be insulated from any possibility of biasing their data or its interpretation by a desire to make things look good. Points usually go to outsiders on this score, although fine evaluation has been done by staff evaluators of scrupulous integrity. It even happens that an outside research firm will sweeten the interpretation of program results (by choice of respondents, by types of statistical tests applied) in order to ingratiate itself with a program and get further contracts. In any event, safeguarding the study against even unintentional bias is important.

Understanding of the program. Knowledge of what is going on in the program is vital for an evaluation staff. They need to know both the real issues facing the agency and the real events that are taking place in the program if their evaluation is to be relevant. It is here that in-house staffs chalk up points, although outsiders too can find out about program proc-

12 See Elmer Luchterhand, "Research and the Dilemmas in Developing Social Programs," in *The Uses of Sociology,* ed. P. F. Lazarsfeld, W. H. Sewell, and H. L. Wilensky (New York: Basic Books, Inc., Publishers, 1967), pp. 513–17; Rensis Likert and Ronald Lippitt, "The Utilization of Social Science," in *Research Methods in the Behavioral Sciences,* ed. Leon Festinger and Daniel Katz (New York: Holt, Rinehart & Winston, Inc., 1953), pp. 581–646; Martin Weinberger, "Evaluating Educational Programs: Observations by a Market Researcher," *Urban Review,* III, No. 4 (1969), 23–26.

esses if they make the effort and are given access to sources of information.

Potential for utilization. Utilization of results often requires that evaluators take an active role in moving from research data to interpretation of the results in a policy context. In-house staff, who are willing to make recommendations on the basis of results and advocate them in agency meetings and conferences, may be better able to secure them a hearing. But sometimes it is outsiders, with their prestige and authority, who are able to induce the agency to pay attention to the evaluation.

Autonomy. Insiders generally take the program's basic assumptions and organizational arrangements as given and conduct their evaluation within the existing framework. The outsider may be able to exercise more autonomy and take a wider perspective. While respecting the formulation of issues set by the program, he may be able to introduce alternatives that are a marked departure from the status quo. The implications he draws from evaluation data may be oriented less to tinkering and more to fundamental restructuring of the program.[13] However, such a broader approach is neither common among outsiders nor unknown among insiders.

All these considerations have to be balanced against each other. There is no one "best site" for evaluation. The agency must weigh the factors afresh in each case and make an estimate of the way which the benefits pile up.

Level in the structure

Whoever actually does the evaluation, the evaluation staff fits somewhere in the organizational bureaucracy. The evaluator reports to a person at some level of authority in the program organization or its supervisory or funding body, and he is responsible to that person and that position for the work he does. If the evaluator is an insider, he reports on a regular basis. The outsider researcher also receives his assignment and reports his results to (and may get intermediate advice from) the holder of a particular organizational position.

The important distinction in organizational location for our discussion is the difference between the policy maker and the program manager. To abridge our earlier catalog of users of evaluation and the decisions they have to make, the key points are these:

[13] Robert K. Merton, "Role of the Intellectual in Public Bureaucracy," in *Social Theory and Social Structure* (New York: The Free Press, 1964), pp. 207–24.

User	*Decision*
Policy maker	Whether to expand, contract, or change the program
Program manager	Which methods, structures, techniques, or staff patterns to use

The evaluation should be placed within the organizational structure at a level consonant with its mission. If it is directed at answering the policy questions (How good is the program overall?), evaluators should report to policy makers. If the basic shape of the program is unquestioned and the evaluation issue centers on variations in specific features, the evaluator should probably be responsible to the program managers.[14]

Real problems arise when the evaluation is inappropriately located in the structure. An evaluation that is initiated by and responsible to program managers is under all kinds of pressure not to come up with findings that disparage the effectiveness of the whole program. If it does, the managers are likely to stall the report at the program level and it will never receive consideration in higher councils.[15] On the other other hand, when top policy makers initiate and oversee the evaluation, their questions are paramount, and questions about operations may get the short end of the budget. Nor do the evaluators have the easy, informal contact with program managers and practitioners that allows them to hear and understand the problems and options they face. It sometimes becomes difficult to study the effectiveness of different program components because staff see the evaluators as "inspectors" checking up on them and become vary of divulging information that might reflect poorly on their performance. Nor are they always cooperative in maintaining the conditions necessary for evaluation research, particularly if there is competition among program levels and the evaluation is viewed as an effort to assert the priorities of the higher level.

The problem of structural location becomes more complex when the evaluation is serving both masters. By and large, it appears best to report in at the higher level. In that way, the evaluator maintains greater autonomy. But then he has to make special efforts to learn enough about critical issues in day-to-day program operations to incorporate them into the study and to maintain the support of local program managers for appropriate research conditions.

[14] This rule of thumb applies whether the evaluation is performed by an in-house evaluation unit or by an outside research organization. Either one should report in at the level of decision to which its work is addressed. The outsiders probably have greater latitude in going around the organizational chain of command and finding access to an appropriate ear, but even they will be circumscribed by improper location.

[15] This point is discussed in Likert and Lippitt, *op. cit.*

Good placement in the structure is important. A recent report by Wholey et al. on federal evaluation practice [16] discusses this issue in terms of federal agencies' responsibilities. It recommends that a central evaluation staff in each agency should have responsibility for planning and coordinating all evaluation work in the department, but that staff at different levels should be responsible for direct supervision of evaluation studies depending on their scope and purpose.

Policy makers are most often called upon to make choices among national programs; program managers are most often called upon to make choices of emphasis or decisions on the future of individual projects *within* national programs. To the extent possible, program impact evaluations, designed to discover the worth of an entire national program, should be directed by persons not immediately involved in management of the program and operation. Program strategy evaluation should be directed by persons close enough to the program to introduce variations into the program.[17]

Wherever the evaluation project sits in the structure, it should have the autonomy that all research requires to report objectively on the evidence and to pursue issues, criteria, and analysis beyond the limits set by the program in order to better understand and interpret the phenomena under study.

[16] Joseph S. Wholey et al., *Federal Evaluation Policy* (Washington, D.C.: The Urban Institute, 1970), pp. 54–71.
[17] *Ibid.*, p. 65.

3

Formulating the Question
and Measuring the Answer

The traditional formulation of the evaluation question is: To what extent is the program succeeding in reaching its goals? Variations are possible: Is program *A* doing better than program *B* in reaching their common goals? How well is the program achieving results *X*, *Y*, and *Z* with groups *F*, *G*, and *H*? Which components of the program (*R*, *S*, or *T*) are having more success? But the basic notion is the same. There are goals; there is a planned activity (or several planned activities) aimed at achieving those goals; there is a measure made of the extent to which the goals are achieved. In evaluation there is also the expectation that controls are set up so that the researcher can tell whether it was the *program* that led to the achievement of goals rather than any outside factors (such as the maturing of the participants, improvement in the economy, and so on). The issue of study design—how controls can be instituted in research on an action program—is the subject of the next chapter.

The evaluation question sounds simple enough in the abstract. All the researcher has to do, it seems, is:

1. Find out the program's goals.

2. Translate the goals into measurable indicators of goal achievement.

3. Collect data on the indicators for those who participated in the program (and for an equivalent control group who did not).

4. Compare the data on participants (and controls) with the goal criteria.

And voilà!

But what looks elementary in theory turns out in practice to be a demanding enterprise. Programs are nowhere near as neat and accommodating as the evaluator expects. Nor are outside circumstances as passive and unimportant as he might like. Whole platoons of unexpected problems spring up. This chapter deals with four:

1. Program goals are often hazy, ambiguous, hard to pin down. Occasionally, the official goals are merely a long list of pious and partly incompatible platitudes.

2. Programs not only move toward official goals. They accomplish other things, sometimes in addition and sometimes instead. The evaluator has a responsibility to take a look at these unexpected consequences of program activities.

3. The program is a congeries of activities, people, and structures. Some of its elements are necessary for the effects it achieves; others are irrelevant baggage. Decision makers want to know what the basic and essential features of the program are, so that (if successful) they can reproduce them or (if unsuccessful) avoid them. How do you identify and separate out the elements that matter?

4. The evaluation question as posed ignores the issue of why the program succeeds or fails. The *why* is often just as important to know as *how well* the program works.

In addressing these issues, we will recommend a series of strategies. Possibly the most important theme (and we return to it in the next chapter when we discuss design) is the classification of the component parts of the program. Each element (of activity, approach, structure, participant, and so on) that is presumed likely to affect outcomes is observed, defined, and classified. The differences that evolve between groups, between activities, and so on give increasing information about what works and does not work in reaching program goals.

In this chapter, then, we consider these core issues:

1. Formulating the program goals that the evaluation will use as criteria
2. Choosing among multiple goals
3. Investigating unanticipated consequences
4. Measuring outcomes

5. Specifying what the program is
6. Measuring program inputs and intervening processes
7. Collecting the necessary data

FORMULATING PROGRAM GOALS

It is a common experience for an evaluator to be called in to study the effects of a program and not be told its purpose. If he presses for a statement of goals, program administrators may answer in terms of the number of people they intend to serve, the kinds of service they will offer, the types of staff they will have, and similar information. For program implementers, these are "program goals" in a real and valid sense, but they are not the primary currency in which the evaluator deals. He is interested in the intended *consequences* of the program. When he pursues the question, "What is the program trying to accomplish?" many program people give fuzzy replies, often global and unrealistic in scope. They may hazard the statement that they are trying to "improve education," "enhance the quality of life," "reduce crime," "strengthen democratic processes." Thus begins the long, often painful, process of getting people to state goals in terms that are *clear, specific,* and *measurable.*

The goal must be clear so that the evaluator knows what to look for. In a classroom program, should he look for evidence of enjoyment of the class? interest in the subject matter? knowledge of the subject matter? use of the subject matter in further problem solving?

The goal has to be specific. It must be able to be translated into operational terms and made visible. Somebody has to *do* something differently when the goal is reached. Thus, if the goal is to interest students in new materials, they are likely to talk more often in class, or raise their hands more often, or do more outside reading on the subject, or tell their parents about it, or any of several other things.

For evaluation purposes, the goal has to be measurable. This is not as serious a restriction as it may seem at first glance. Once goal statements are clear and unambiguous, skilled researchers can measure all manner of things. They can use the whole arsenal of research techniques—observation, content analysis of documents, testing, search of existing records, interviews, questionnaires, sociometric choices, laboratory experiments, game playing, physical examinations, measurement of physical evidence, and so on. With attitude tests and opinion polls, they can measure even such relatively "soft" goals as improvements in self-esteem or self-reliance. But since few programs set out only to change attitudes, the evaluator will also want to find and measure the behavioral consequences of changed attitudes—the things participants do because they feel different about themselves, other people, or the situation.

Some programs find it extremely difficult to formulate goals in these terms. David Kallen tells of working with an advisory committee to plan for evaluation of a detached worker program for gang youth. Asked to specify the program's goals, the committee members came up with such things as improving the behavior of the youth, helping them become better citizens, and improving their school work. When they tried to translate the goals into operational criteria of program success, "behavior" and "citizenship" were too vague to use, and school grades were too likely to be influenced by teachers' stereotyped perceptions of the youngsters. The discouraging story continues:

> Finally, it turned out that a number of the area residents objected to the young people's use of swear words, and it was decided that one measure of behavioral improvement would be the reduction in swearing, and that this was something the detached worker should aim for in his interaction with the youngsters he was working with. [Was the group identifying program goals or making up new ones?] It was therefore agreed that part of the criteria of success would be a reduction in swearing. I might add that this was the only measure of success upon which the evaluation team and the program advisory committee could agree.[1]

Fuzziness of program goals is a common enough phenomenon to warrant attention. Part of the explanation probably lies in practitioners' concentration on concrete matters of program functioning and their pragmatic mode of operation. They often have an intuitive rather than an analytic approach to program development. But there is also a sense in which ambiguity serves a useful function: It may mask underlying divergences in intent. Support from many quarters is required to get a program off the ground, and the glittering generalities that pass for goal statements are meant to satisfy a variety of interests and perspectives.

However, when there is little consensus on what a program is trying to do, the staff may be working at cross-purposes. One side benefit of evaluation is to focus attention on the formulation of goals in terms of the specific behaviors that program practitioners aim to achieve. The effort may force disagreements into the open and lead to conflict. But if differences can be reconciled (and the program may not be viable if they are not), the clarification can hardly help but rationalize program implementation. It may reveal discrepancies between program goals and program

---

[1] Personal letter from David J. Kallen, January 10, 1966.

content, in which case either the content or, as Berlak notes,[2] the goal statement should be changed. When a sense of common purpose is reached, the logic and rationality of practice are likely to be enhanced.

What does an evaluator do when he is faced with a program that cannot agree on a statement of specific and meaningful goals? Four courses are open to him:

1. He can pose the question and wait for program personnel to reach a consensus. But as Freeman and Sherwood[3] note, he should bring books to the office to read while waiting for them to agree. And they still may not develop a statement that provides an adequate basis for evaluation.

2. Another thing he can do is read everything about the program he can find, talk to practitioners at length, observe the program in operation, and then sit down and frame the statement of goals himself. Sometimes this is a reasonable procedure, but there are two dangers. One is that he may read his own professional preconceptions into the program and subtly shift the goals (and the ensuing study) in the direction of his own interests. The other risk is that when the study is completed, the program practitioners will dismiss the results with the comment, "But that's not really what we were trying to do at all."

3. He can set up a collaborative effort in goal formulation. This is probably the best approach. Sitting with the program people, the evaluator can offer successive approximations of goal statements. The program staff modifies them, and the discussion continues until agreement is reached.

4. He can table the question of goals, and enter not upon evaluation in the traditional sense, but on a more exploratory, open-ended study. In complex and uncharted areas, this may be a better strategy than formulating arbitrary and superficial "goals" in order to get on with the study while the really significant happenings around the program are allowed to take place unstudied, unanalyzed, and unsung. Evaluations based on too-specific goals and indicators of success may be premature in a field in which there is little agreement on what constitutes success.[4]

[2] Harold Berlak, "Values, Goals, Public Policy and Educational Evaluation," *Review of Educational Research,* XL, No. 2 (1970), 261–78.

[3] Howard E. Freeman and Clarence C. Sherwood, "Research in Large-scale Intervention Programs," *Journal of Social Issues,* XXI, No. 1 (1965), 11–28.

[4] See Cyril S. Belshaw, "Evaluation of Technical Assistance as a Contribution to Development," *International Development Review,* VIII (1966), 2–6, 23, for a situation in which this was the case. He goes on, however, to recommend a theoretical framework and a series of possible criteria of success for technical assistance programs, such as an increase in the range of commodities produced or increased division of labor. He offers an approximation of goal statements that can be progressively modified by other researchers, operators, and scholars.

The experienced evaluator also searches for the hidden agenda, the covert goals of the project that are unlikely to be articulated, but whose achievement sometimes determines success or failure no matter what else happens. For example, if a program of interdisciplinary studies in a university fails to win the support of the departmental faculties and the university administration, even consummate educational results may not be enough to keep it alive. The evaluator, if he is to study the attainment of goals, is well advised to keep an eye on the "system" goals (those that help maintain the viability of the program in its environment) as well as the "outcome" goals. He will learn much that explains why the program makes the adaptations it does and where the real game is.[5]

Some researchers have even proposed that the goal model of evaluation should be junked in favor of a system model.[6] The elements of such a model are not yet clear; there are almost as many interpretations as there are participants in the discussion. But the common recognition is that organizations pursue other functions besides the achievement of official goals. They have to acquire resources, coordinate subunits, and adapt to the environment. These preoccupations get entangled with, and set limits to, attainment of program goals. According to system model proponents, an evaluation that ignores them is likely to result in artificial and perhaps misleading conclusions.

What would a system model look like? Etzioni, and Schulberg and Baker suggest that the system model should be based on the evaluator's extensive knowledge of the organization and his understanding of the optimal allocation of resources among organization-maintenance and goal-achievement functions. The key question then becomes: "Under the given conditions, how close does the organizational allocation of resources approach an optimum distribution?"[7] Provocative as the notion is, it sets

[5] Andrew C. Fleck, Jr. "Evaluation Research Programs in Public Health Practice," *Annals of the New York Academy of Science,* CVII, No. 2 (1963), 717–24, recommends that evaluators have intimate knowledge of the organization and its relative emphasis on short-run stability versus long-run survival.

[6] See Edward A. Suchman, "Action for What? A Critique of Evaluative Research," in *The Organization, Management, and Tactics of Social Research,* ed. Richard O'Toole (Cambridge, Mass.: Schenkman Publishing Co., 1970); Amitai Etzioni, "Two Approaches to Organizational Analysis: A Critique and a Suggestion," *Administrative Science Quarterly,* V, No. 2 (1960), 257–78; Herbert C. Schulberg and Frank Baker, "Program Evaluation Models and the Implementation of Research Findings," *American Journal of Public Health,* LVIII, No. 7 (1968), 1248–55; Perry Levinson, "Evaluation of Social Welfare Programs: Two Research Models," *Welfare in Review,* IV, No. 10 (1966), 5–12; Herbert C. Schulberg, Alan Sheldon, and Frank Baker, "Introduction" in *Program Evaluation in the Health Fields* (New York: Behavioral Publications Inc., 1970).

[7] Etzioni, *op. cit.,* p. 262.

such demanding requirements for the evaluator (knowing more about the organization than the organization knows itself) that it is difficult to imagine its practical application, at least in these terms. Perhaps future development will bring its genuine insights into the realm of practicality. For the time being, most evaluators will probably stick with the goal model, which is certainly justifiable on its own grounds, and give as much attention to the organizational and community systems that affect the program as the situation seems to warrant.

Choices Among Goals

Once the goals of the project are clearly, specifically, and behaviorally defined, the next step is to decide which of them to evaluate. How does the evaluator make the decision?

Usability and practicality

Part of the answer lies in the potential for utilization. How will the evaluation findings be applied, and which goals are relevant to that decision? Part of the answer lies in the hard realities of time, money, and access. How far off in time the evaluator can study is limited by how long the project—and the evaluation—last; how much he can study is at least partly a function of money; whether he can examine certain classes of effects depends on whether he is permitted access to people and agencies. A tendency endemic in all kinds of research is to study what is easy to study rather than what ought to be studied. It is particularly important for the evaluator to avoid this kind of cop-out and to concentrate on key concerns of the program.

Relative importance

There remains still another factor—the relative importance of different goals. This requires value judgment, and the program's own priorities are critical. The evaluator will have to press to find out priorities—which goals the staff sees as critical to its mission and which are subsidiary. But since the evaluator is not a mere technician for the translation of a program's stated aims into measurement instruments, he has a responsibility to express his own interpretation of the relative importance of goals. He doesn't want to do an elaborate study on the attainment of minor and innocuous goals, while vital goals go unexplored.[8]

Incompatibilities

In some cases there are incompatibilities among stated goals. A model cities program, for example, seeks to increase coordination among the public and private agencies serving its run-down neighborhood. It also desires innovation, the contrivance of unusual new approaches to services for the poor residents. Clearly, coordination among agencies will be easier around old, established, accepted patterns of service than around new ones. Innovation is likely to weaken coordination, and coordination is likely to dampen the innovating spirit. Which goal is more "real"? Evaluation cannot stick its head in the sand and treat the two goals as equal and independent.

Short-term or long-term goals?

Another issue is whether short- or long-term goals are more important. Decision makers, who by professional habit respond to the demands of the budget cycle rather than the research cycle, usually want quick answers. If they have to make a decision in time for next year's budget, there is little value in inquiring into the durability of effects over 24 months. It is this year's results that count.

But decision makers can often be persuaded to see the utility of continuing an investigation over several years, so that the program's long-term effectiveness becomes manifest. Clearly, it is good to know whether early changes persist, or on the other hand, whether the absence of early change reflects a "sleeper effect," the slow building up of important changes over time. Evaluations, wherever possible, should look into long-term effects, particularly when basic policies or costly facilities are at stake. A comparison of short- *and* long-term effects provides additional information about how, and at what pace, effects take place.

The evaluator is well-advised to thrash out the final selection of goals for study with decision makers and program managers. They are all involved. It is he who will have to live with the study and they who will have to live with the study results and—one would hope—their implementation.

[8] Robert E. Stake discusses the evaluator's responsibility for evaluating proffered goals. "The Countenance of Educational Evaluation," *Teachers College Record,* LXVIII, No. 7 (1967), 523–40.

Yardsticks

Once the goals are set, the next question is how much progress toward the goal marks success. Suppose a vocational program enrolls 400, graduates 200, places 100 on jobs, of whom 50 are still working three months later. Is this success? Would 100 be success? 200? 25? Without direction on this issue, interpreters can alibi any set of data. A tiny change is better than no change at all. No change is better than (expected) retrogression. Different people looking at the same data can come up with different conclusions in the tradition of the "fully-only" school of analysis. "Fully 25 percent of the students . . ." boasts the promoter; "only 25 percent of the students . . ." sighs the detractor.

Only on a comparative basis does the question really make sense. How do the results compare with last year's results, with the results for those who did not get the special program, or better still, with the results from programs with similar intent? [9] If comparable data are not available, the evaluator can present his results and let others draw their own conclusions. Or he can get into the act by drawing on past experience, the opinions of administrators and staff, and perhaps outside experts, in reaching a judgment of his own.[10] Early attention to standards of judgment—before the data come in—can forestall later wrangling.

Unanticipated Consequences

The program has desired goals. There is also the possibility that it will have consequences that it did not intend. The discussion of unanticipated results usually carries the gloomy connotation of undesirable results, but there can also be unexpected good results and some that are a mixture of good and bad.

Undesirable effects can come about for a variety of reasons. Sometimes the program is poorly conceived and exacerbates the very conditions it

[9] This of course limits the question rather than settles it. How *much* better must the program be before it is considered a success? Statistically significant differences do not necessarily mean substantive significance. Perhaps cost-benefit analysis brings the wisest question to bear: How much does it cost for each given amount of improvement? Carol H. Weiss, "Planning an Action Project Evaluation," in *Learning in Action,* ed. June L. Shmelzer (Washington, D.C.: Government Printing Office, 1966), pp. 15–16.

[10] Stake, *op. cit.,* pp. 527, 536–38, suggests comparisons with absolute standards, with other programs, and with the opinions of experts for judgment of success.

aimed to alleviate. A loan program to inefficient small businessmen may only get them deeper into debt. Or a program can boomerang by bringing to light woes that have long been accepted. Some programs raise people's expectations. If progress is too slow or if only a few people benefit, the results may be widespread frustration and bitterness. Occasionally, a program that invades the territory of existing agencies generates anger, competition, and a bureaucratic wrangle that lowers the effectiveness of services.

Good unanticipated consequences are not so usual, because reformers trying to sell a new program are likely to have listed and exhausted all the positive results possible. Nevertheless, there are occasions when a program has a happy spin-off, such as having its successful features taken over by a program in a different field. There can be spillovers of good program results to other aspects of a program participant's life. For example, pupils who learn reading skills may become more cooperative and less disruptive or aggressive in school and at home. Contagion effects appear, too. People who never attended the program learn the new ideas or behaviors through contact with those who did.

Sometimes programs tackle one aspect of a complex problem. Even if they achieve good results in their area, the more important effect may be to throw the original system out of kilter. Thus an assistance program to underdeveloped areas introduces a new strain of rice that increases crop yield—the goal of the program. But at the same time, the effect is to make the rich farmers richer (because they can afford the new seed and fertilizer and can afford to take risks), widen the gulf between them and the subsistence farmers, and lead to social and political unrest. Fragmented programs all too often fail to take into account interrelationships between program efforts and the overall system in which people function. What are originally conceived as good results in one sphere may be dysfunctional in the longer view. It is because of such complex interlinkages that the notion of a systems approach to evelution is appealing.

The evaluator has to keep an eye on the "other" consequences of the program he is studying. Although decision makers have not articulated them as goals, he must unearth and study consequences that have significant impact on people and systems. Like the formulation of goals, this exercise requires thought and attention. A wise evaluator brainstorms in advance about all the effects, good, bad, and indifferent, that could flow from the program. Envisioning the worst as well as the best of all possible worlds, he makes plans for keeping tabs on the range of likely outcomes. What were "unanticipated consequences" are now—if he judged well—unintended but anticipated. He also has to remain flexible and open enough to spot the emergence of effects that even his sweeping imagination had not envisioned.

If he or his evaluation staff is close enough to the scene to observe what goes on, informal observation may be sufficient for the first look at unplanned effects. In more remote or complex situations, he will have to develop measures and data-gathering instruments to pull in the requisite information. Once trends become clear and side effects are seen to be a strong possibility, he will want as precise measures as he can devise of what may become the most important elements in the program field. He never wants to be caught saying, "The program (on our outcome measures) was a success, but the patient died."

Measurement: Indicators
of Outcomes

After the specific goals have been selected for study, the evaluator's next step is the development of *indicators* to measure the extent to which they are achieved. These indicators of program outcomes are the *dependent* variables of the study.

The evaluator is concerned too, with the description and measure of other factors. There are the relevant aspects of the program—the inputs— which are the *independent* variables of the study. There may also be *intervening* variables, factors that mediate between inputs and outcomes. These two types of measures are discussed in a later section of this chapter.

Developing measures

The development of measures, sometimes referred to as "instrumentation," is a demanding phase of the evaluation. If the evaluator is lucky, and earlier studies have been done in the field or measures have been created that are suitable for the subject of his concern, the task becomes one of locating existing measures. It is worth a fair amount of searching to locate measures that have already proved workable, rather than to create new ones. Much of the trial and error work is done. Also, it is generally possible to find out the responses that earlier investigators derived through the use of these measures, and thus to have available some kinds of comparative data from another population. Comparison helps to pinpoint the characteristics of the evaluation group that are "special" and the extent of their divergence from other groups.

Repeated use of common measures helps to build up a body of knowledge. As different evaluation studies use common indicators of outcome (for example, scores on the same test), it becomes possible to begin to make comparisons about the relative effectiveness of one program against another. (The important qualification is that other factors have to be considered, and preferably be constant, if the judgments are to be fair.) In recent years, several handbooks of tried and tested measures have been published as guides for researchers. The distribution of responses from previous research is often included. See, for example:

Charles M. Bonjean, Richard J. Hill, and S. Dale McLemore, *Sociological Measurement: An Inventory of Scales and Indices* (San Francisco, Calif.: Chandler, 1967).

Oscar Buros, *Mental Measurements Yearbook,* 6th ed. (Highland Park, N.J.: Gryphon Press, 1965).

————, *Personality Tests and Reviews* (Highland Park, N.J.: Gryphon Press, 1970).

Delbert C. Miller, *Handbook of Research Design and Social Measurement* (New York: McKay, 1964).

John P. Robinson, Jerrold G. Rusk, and Kendra B. Head, *Measures of Political Attitudes* (Ann Arbor, Mich.: Survey Research Center, University of Michigan, 1968).

John P. Robinson and Phillip R. Shaver, *Measures of Social Psychological Attitudes* (Ann Arbor, Mich.: Survey Research Center, University of Michigan, 1969).

John P. Robinson, A. Athanasiou, and Kendra B. Head, *Measures of Occupational Attitudes and Occupational Characteristics* (Ann Arbor, Mich.: Survey Research Center, University of Michigan, 1967).

Marvin E. Shaw and Jack M. Wright, *Scales for the Measurement of Attitudes* (New York: McGraw-Hill Book Company, 1967).

U.S. Bureau of the Budget, Executive Office of the President, *Household Survey Manual 1969.* Gives concepts, definitions, and questions used by federal statistical agencies.

Frequently, for all the assiduity of his search, the evaluator finds no measures directly relevant to the subjects he wants to study.[11] He may find some that are inferentially related, and if they are easy to collect, long-used, or have known distributions, he may be tempted to make do with them. For example, one evaluator wants to know whether mothers who participated in a parents' program become more permissive in raising their children. Let us say that he finds a tolerance inventory, a personality test that has been normed on groups similar to his and includes items on acceptance

---

[11] Hemphill suggests that "pure researchers" develop better measures and better conceptualizations for the evaluator to use. John K. Hemphill, "The Relationship Between Research and Evaluation Studies," in *Educational Evaluation: New Roles, New Means, 68 Yearbook of the National Society for the Study of Education,* ed. Ralph W. Tyler (Chicago: National Society for the Study of Education, 1969), Chap. IX.

of deviant behavior. Should he use the mothers' scores on this test as an indicator of increased permissiveness in child rearing? The main assumptions he has to make are (1) that the quality of "tolerance" that the inventory measures is the same dimension as the one reflected in child-rearing permissiveness and (2) that written answers to the inventory questions are a true reflection of mothers' actual behaviors.

It is usually wiser to stick to the relevant core of the subject under study than to rely on a string of unproved assumptions. Developing new measures can be difficult and time-consuming, but measures that are off-center from the main issue, even when reputable and time-honored, are likely to be of little use at all.

Devising questions, test items, and forms often looks so easy that it comes as a shock to find how many people fail to understand or misinterpret even seemingly simple items. Before embarking on the development of new measures, the investigator should have an acquaintance with considerations of validity and reliability. (See Section III of the Bibliography for a number of references on measurement.) Careful conceptualization and definition are called for, and questions have to be pre-tested and revised (often several times around) until it is clear that they are bringing in the desired information.

Multiple measures

Adequate indicators of success in evaluation, like adequate measures of concepts in all social research, usually entail multiple measurement. Each specific measure is an approximation of the outcome in which we are really interested. Say we are concerned with good driving as the outcome of a course in driver education. Knowledge of traffic rules can be one measure; ratings of driving ability by an observer might be another; records of traffic violations, a third. At best, each is a partial measure encompassing a fraction of the larger concept.[12] On occasion, its link to the real outcome is problematic and tenuous. Moreover, each measure contains a load of irrelevant superfluities, "extra baggage" unrelated to the outcomes under study. By the use of a number of measures, each contributing a different facet of information, we can limit the effect of irrelevancies and develop a more rounded and truer picture of program outcomes.[13]

[12] Amitai Etzioni and Edward Lehman, "Some Dangers in 'Valid' Social Measurement," *Annals of the American Academy of Political and Social Science,* Vol. 373 (September 1967), 1–15.

[13] Donald T. Campbell and Julian C. Stanley, "Experimental and Quasi-experimental Designs for Research on Teaching," in *Handbook of Research on Teaching,* ed. N. L. Gage (Chicago: Rand McNally & Co., 1963), pp. 203–4.

Multiple measures might be useful, for example, in the evaluation of educational curriculums. Evaluators have usually relied on formal tests of pupil achievement. But test scores are influenced by many things other than the cogency of the curriculum, and the curriculum is intended to produce understandings and applications of knowledge that are only partially susceptible to assessment by tests. Cronbach suggests the need for measures of classroom behavior, attitudes, and the subsequent careers of students.[14]

Separate measures can be combined to form one overall measure of program success. This requires some assurance that the different measures are complementary and not repetitions of the same dimension. Further, it requires decisions on the relative importance of the different measures (Do they deserve equal billing?) and on the statistical procedures to represent the relative values of measures that use different scales (How do you combine reading scores and numbers of books borrowed from the library?). There is also the possibility that a composite index masks the upward and downward movement of the separate indicators. Therefore, even when an index is a useful device, the evaluator will want to report changes in the separate measures as well.

Proximate measures

Sometimes the real changes that a program wants to produce lie far in the future and are not so much "goals" as unanalyzed pious hopes. A management incentive program aims to increase the organization's attraction for executives in the interests of improved long-term managerial effectiveness; an educational program for inner-city children is intended to improve their school performance in order to enhance their social and economic status as adults. It would take years, even decades, to test the program's effectiveness in achieving its long-range expectations. In the interim, proxy measures have to be used that are germane to more immediate goals and presumably linked to desired ultimate outcomes, for example, length of executive tenure, or children's scores on achievement tests. Unfortunately, there is often little research evidence that the purported relationships hold —for example, that tenure is associated with management effectiveness or that school achievement is directly related to the economic and social advancement of the poor.[15] Nor does existing knowledge always suggest better proximate measures.

[14] Lee J. Cronbach, "Evaluation for Course Improvement," *Teachers College Record,* LXIV, No. 8 (1963), 672–83.

[15] David K. Cohen, "Politics and Research: Evaluation of Social Action Programs in Education," *Review of Educational Research,* XL, No. 2 (1970), 218–19.

The problem affects not only evaluation; it is also central to program design. Programs have to be designed to produce certain short-term changes on the assumption that they are necessary conditions for achieving long-range ends. As in many other aspects, the evaluation inherits the fallibilities of the program. Often the best that evaluation can do, at least under the usual time constraints and in the absence of better knowledge, is accept the program's assumptions and find out how well near-term goals are being met. It is left to further research to explore the relationships between short-term goals and long-term consequences. This solution-by-retreat lacks heroic grandeur, but in many cases it represents the only feasible way to get on with the evaluative job.

But when desired consequences are not so remote as to outlast the evaluation, there are decided advantages in measuring both the short-term and longer-range effects. Programs attempt to set in motion a sequence of events expected to achieve desired goals. As Suchman has noted,[16] if the program is unsuccessful, there are two general categories of reasons. Either it did not activate the "causal process" that would have culminated in the intended goals (this is a failure of program), or it may have set the presumed "causal process" in motion but the process did not "cause" the desired effects (this is a failure of theory). (See Figure 3–1.)

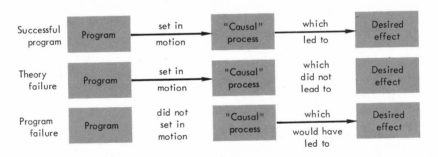

FIG. 3–1. Types of program failure.

Stated another way, program failure is a failure to achieve proximate goals; theory failure occurs when the achievement of proximate goals does not lead to final desired outcomes.

When previous research has demonstrated the link between immediate program goals and desired long-term outcomes, there is little need for evaluation to pursue results beyond the first stage. In evaluation of a Smokers'

[16] Edward A. Suchman, "Evaluating Educational Programs: A Symposium," *Urban Review*, III, No. 4 (1969), 16.

Clinic, it is probably enough to discover that the program led participants to stop smoking. It is not essential to investigate the ultimate incidence of lung cancer. But in fields where knowledge is less developed, further investigation is highly desirable.

Knowing only that intended effects were not achieved is not instructive for future program planning. The availability of short-term and long-term measures would help to indicate whether this was a result of program failure or theory failure.[17] By examining the association between immediate effects and long-range consequences, evaluation can contribute to program practice and program planning—and also to the development of social theory.

Types of measures

Measures that are useful for assessing outcomes in evaluation research depend on program intent. They can deal with attitudes, values, knowledge, behavior, budgetary allocations, agency service patterns, productivity, and many other items. They can relate to the people being served, the agencies offering service or those affected by changed patterns of service, the neighborhood or the community, or the public at large.

Measuring effects on persons served. Most evaluations tend to concentrate on changes in program participants. They commonly use measures of attitudes, values, personality variables, knowledge, and skills. Each of these may be directly relevant to program goals. A vocational education program, for example, may expect to impart basic knowledge, specific skills,

---

[17] There is a body of research on the ineffectiveness of counseling and group therapy programs for delinquents and inmates, some of which attempts to cope with this issue. See, for example, H. J. Meyer, E. F. Borgatta, and W. C. Jones, *Girls at Vocational High* (New York: Russell Sage Foundation, 1965); Walter B. Miller, "The Impact of a 'Total-Community' Delinquency Control Project," *Social Problems,* X, No. 2 (1962), 168–91; H. Ashley Weeks, *Youthful Offenders at Highfields* (Ann Arbor, Mich.: University of Michigan Press, 1958); Edwin Powers and Helen Witmer, *An Experiment in the Prevention of Delinquency: The Cambridge-Somerville Youth Study* (New York: Columbia University Press, 1951); William McCord and Joan McCord, *Origins of Crime: A New Evaluation of the Cambridge-Somerville Youth Study* (New York: Columbia University Press, 1969); Gene Kassebaum, David Ward, and Daniel Wilner, *Prison Treatment and Parole Survival: An Empirical Assessment* (New York: John Wiley & Sons, Inc., 1971); William C. Berleman and Thomas W. Steinburn, "The Execution and Evaluation of a Delinquency Prevention Program," *Social Problems,* XIV, No. 4 (1967), 413–23; Nathan Caplan, "Treatment Intervention and Reciprocal Interaction Effects," *Journal of Social Issues,* XXIV, No. 1 (1968), 63–88.

values about work, and certain attitudes toward the job. The usual sources of data are tests, questionnaires, and interviews.

Most programs intend to change overt behavior as well. Information on behavior can be collected through self-reports of the individuals in the program or reports by people who know them (teachers, parents, employers). In some settings, behavior can be observed. Records are another source of information for such items as school grades, arrests, earnings, or hospital admissions.

In the past, evaluators tended to rely heavily on the attitudinal and knowledge measures that were easy to obtain and sidestep the collection of the more difficult behavioral data. But the real payoff for programs is usually a change in behavior. Since it is dubious that changes in attitude or knowledge are necessary and sufficient conditions for behavioral change, the evaluator is well advised to proceed into the behavioral realm.[18] It may be a matter of interest to investigate the extent to which attitudinal or knowledge change is an intervening variable, that is, a link to the dependent variable of behavioral change (see Figure 3–2).

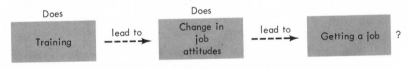

FIG. 3–2. Measuring behavioral change: a hypothesis in diagram form.

All too frequently, behavioral outcome measures are not directly available. How, for example, do you observe, record, and quantify a decrease in neurotic behavior? The measurement problems are staggering. In many such cases, the evaluator turns to expert judgments. Experts can rate the patient on a scale from "very much improved" to "very much worse."

When judgments are being used as indicators of outcome, a number of precautions are called for. First, it is usually advisable to have outsiders, rather than the program staff, do the rating. However objective they are, staff members can be suspected of bias—often justly—in the direction of

---

[18] The reverse point, that measure of gross behavioral change is incomplete without knowledge of intrapsychic variables, is made by Leonard A. Kogan and Ann W. Shyne, "Tender-minded and Tough-minded Approaches in Evaluation Research," *Welfare in Review,* IV, No. 2 (1966), 12–17.

seeing improvement where none exists, or placing high value on tiny, subtle shifts that seem trivial to others. Another precaution is the use of several judges, each rating the same cases, to see how much consistency (reliability) there is between judgments. If interrater reliability is low, the whole procedure is suspect and should be revised. Finally, raters need clear direction, and perhaps training, in the factors to consider and their relative importance. Only when they are each applying the same yardstick, and doing so in terms the evaluator has defined, will their ratings have much meaning.[19]

Participants' opinions about the program are sometimes used as an "outcome" measure. They are asked whether they liked it, whether it helped them, whether they would recommend it to others, and similar questions. There is some merit in finding out whether the program appealed to its audience. In the extreme case, if it is totally unacceptable, nobody will come. But certainly people may like or dislike a program for reasons unconnected with its goals. They may have hazy or misguided expectations of what the program is intended to accomplish and therefore assess its interest and utility in irrelevant terms. Unless it is a specific goal of the program to interest or entertain or offer expected services to the participants, the popularity contest model for evaluation is woefully incomplete.[20]

Measuring effects on agencies. Some programs aim to produce changes in institutions rather than in people. They may seek to make local bureaucracies more responsive to residents, alter the type of clientele served or the composition of governing boards, broaden an agency's concept of its mission. In this case, indicators of program outcome will be measures of institutional characteristics. Some of these can be aggregated from data about individuals in the organization (for example, percentage with daily contact with local residents), and some can be global measures of the in-

---

[19] See Robert B. McIntyre and Calvin C. Nelson, "Empirical Evaluation of Instructional Materials," *Educational Technology*, IX, No. 2 (1969), 24–27. They recommend that expert judgments about instructional materials be supplemented by field evaluations of the effects of the materials in actual situations. An interesting use of expert judgment in a field where behavioral data are hard to come by is the medical audit of professional performance; see Mildred Morehead, "The Medical Audit as an Operational Tool," *American Journal of Public Health*, LVII, No. 9 (1967), 1643–56.

[20] Studies of compensatory education programs find one "universal finding": Regardless of the type of program, duration, or actual results, parents are enthusiastic. Edward L. McDill, Mary S. McDill, and J. Timothy Sprehe, *Strategies for Success in Compensatory Education: An Appraisal of Evaluation Research* (Baltimore, Md.: The Johns Hopkins Press, 1969), pp. 43–44. See also Donald T. Campbell, "Reforms as Experiments," *American Psychologist*, XXIV, No. 4 (1969) on the "grateful testimonial," 426.

stitution (for example, total budget, proportion of the budget devoted to a particular activity, hours during which facilities are open). A useful guide to measures on institutions is Allen H. Barton, *Organizational Measurement.*[21]

In some fields, such as education and public health, there has been a tradition of using "checklist" items developed by experts as "standards of service" as the criterion measures for evaluation. These are generally not outcome measures, but statements of popularly accepted "good practice" (teacher-student ratio, adequacy of equipment). Such measures have been useful for purposes of monitoring an agency's activities, for accreditation, and for educating staff and public about service criteria, but they are not the measures with which evaluation research is primarily concerned, since they relate to program input rather than to outcome. As we will see in the next section, measures of this kind may be useful as intervening variables, indices of particular program features that are presumed to have a beneficial effect on outcomes, to mediate between the program and its effects. Evaluation provides an opportunity to *test* whether supposed "good-practice" components of a program *are* in fact related to successful outcomes.

Measuring effects on larger systems. There are occasional programs whose goals are to make changes in a whole network of agencies (increase communication and referral among all agencies dealing with troubled youth in a community) or to change a community or even a national service delivery system (education, mental health, job training). In such cases, inventive measures must be devised. Data can come from interviews with leaders; observations within departments or at meetings; collected statistics on clientele, budgets, housing starts; logs kept by staff; analysis of documents or of news stories; sample surveys of the public; and so on. There has not been much evaluation at this "macro" level, but the possibilities are intriguing.

Measuring effects on the public. If a program seeks to alter public values or attitudes, the appropriate indicator of outcome is obviously the public's views. Elaine and John Cumming, for example, administered questionnaires and conducted interviews to determine the effects of a community educational program designed to alter public views about mental illness.[22]

[21] Princeton, N.J.: College Entrance Examination Board, 1961.

[22] Elaine Cumming and John Cumming, *Closed Ranks: Study of Mental Health Education* (Cambridge, Mass.: Harvard University Press, 1957). The six-month program produced virtually no change in the population's attitudes toward mental illness or the mentally ill.

Specification of the Program

Just as important as conceptualizing the desired outcomes is conceptualizing the nature of the program. What is this program that the evaluator is studying—this amalgam of dreams and personalities, rooms and theories, paper clips and organizational structure, clients and activities, budget and photocopies and great intentions?

Social programs are complex undertakings. Social program evaluators look with something akin to jealousy at evaluators in agriculture who evaluate a new strain of wheat or evaluators in medicine who evaluate the effects of a new drug. These are physical things you can see, touch, and—above all—replicate. The same stimulus can be produced again, and other researchers can study its consequences—under the same or different conditions, with similar or different subjects, but with some assurance that they are looking at the effects of the same *thing*.

Social programs are not nearly so specific. They incorporate a range of components, styles, people, and procedures. It becomes difficult to describe what "the program" really is. In some cases, a program can be expressed in terms that appear clear and reproducible; for example, a new mathematics curriculum, a change in highway speed limits, a decrease in the size of probation officers' caseloads. But the content of the program, what actually goes on, is much harder to describe. There are often marked internal variations in operation from day to day and from staff member to staff member. When you consider a program as large and amorphous as the poverty program or the model cities program, it takes a major effort to just describe and analyze the program input.

Why should the evaluator be concerned with program input? Haven't we noted earlier that his job is to find out whether the program (whatever it is) is achieving its goals? Does it make any difference to his work whether the program is using rote drill, psychoanalysis, or black magic? There are evaluators who are sympathetic to such an approach. They see the program as a "black box," the contents of which do not concern them; they are charged with discovering effects. But if the evaluator has no idea of what the program really is, he may fail to ask the right questions. Perhaps because he believes the inflated barrage of program propaganda, he expects mountain-moving outcomes from what are really puny efforts. More likely, he looks for the wrong order of effects. He looks for the attainment of the types of goals that have been verbalized, when the main resources of the operating program have been invested in a different course of action. (If it aimed to teach blacks and ends up directing its attention at whites, is this a course of a different color?)

Furthermore, unless there is some reasonably accurate and coherent definition of the program, the evaluator does not know to what to attribute the outcomes he observes.[23] Let's remember that evaluation is designed to help with decision making. Decision makers need to know what it was that worked or didn't work, what it is that should be adopted throughout the system or modified. Unless the evaluation can provide evidence on the nature of the program as it existed (not merely on the program as described by practitioners), there is little basis for decision.[24] In an extreme case, when a program is a smashing success and forty communities want to adopt it forthwith, what is it that we tell them to adopt?

The evaluator has to discover the reality of the program rather than its illusion. If he accepts the description given in the application for funds or in publicity releases, he may be evaluating a phantom. He will be attributing effects (or "no effects") to a program that never took place at all, or to one that operated at so low a level of competence or in such a different manner that it hardly deserves to be called by the program name. For example, teachers who are supposed to be using new curriculum materials may not have received them or may not be following the instructions for their use. A recreation program for school children may be closed on weekends when children have free time; it may be closed erratically so that the children get discouraged from attending; it may be offering activities that fail to attract participants. It will hardly be necessary to collect data on the "effects" of these programs, because there is little or no input. Similarly, Hyman and Wright cite the example of a rural health program in Egypt. The investigators checking on the staffing of the program found that most of the health centers lacked vital categories of personnel, and that even the people who were employed were putting in relatively few man-hours of work. Thus they could hardly be providing the kind and scope of services intended.[25]

It takes collection of systematic information and/or observation to find out what is actually taking place. If the program stimulus is well understood and coherent, a few rough measures are sufficient. TB X-rays are

---

[23] Even if the program is clearly described and defined, the evaluator may not be able to make precise statements of causality, but he at least will know where to look for effects and have a running start.

[24] Coleman suggests that there is often a difference between inputs as offered and inputs as received. The loss of input between its disbursement by authorities and its receipt by pupils may be an explanatory variable in analyzing the effectiveness of educational programs. James S. Coleman in "Evaluating Educational Programs: A Symposium," *Urban Review*, III, No. 4 (1969), 6–8.

[25] Herbert H. Hyman and Charles Wright, "Evaluating Social Action Programs," in *The Uses of Sociology*, ed. P. F. Lazarsfeld, W. H. Sewell, and H. L. Wilensky (New York: Basic Books, Inc., Publishers, 1967), p. 745.

TB X-rays, and it is probably enough to know where and to whom they are offered. But if the program is vague or novel or being developed as it goes along, the evaluator may need to describe what is going on. A community mental health center is offering "mental health counseling" to clients, but what exactly does this mean? It may take some digging to find out whether this is referral to psychiatric services, psychotherapy of one type or another, moralizing sermons, referring the client to a job, or any of a dozen other things. Procedures for monitoring the program have to be established. These can be as simple as a discussion with the director, a review of staff records, or attendance at staff meetings, or they can entail interviews with staff or even frequent observation of the program in process. With appropriate sampling procedures, we can characterize even programs that extend widely in space and time.

In most cases, a few relevant descriptive categories suffice to capture the essence of the program. These might include the type of service given, its conceptual emphasis, the type of staff, the setting, and the organizational auspices. If the program is exceedingly complex or differs strikingly from expected patterns, more detail is warranted. Hyman and Wright warn against spending too much time on overelaborating program description; after an initial check to see that the program is really happening and a basic conceptualization, they suggest that the evaluator get on with the job of studying outcomes.[26] But circumstances differ. One program's overelaboration is another program's clarification. More precision is obviously called for when program inputs *vary*. Some clients get one type of service, and others get something different. Under these circumstances, program variables (variables are by definition things that vary) require further attention.

Measurement: Input Variables and Intervening Variables

Not everyone encounters the same experiences within a program. Just as there are outcome variables, so there are program variables. Some participants in a group therapy program attend every session; others attend irregularly. Some receive the attention of experienced therapists; others, of relative novices. There are same-sex groups and both-sex groups, groups in the hospital and groups in the community, psychoanalytically-oriented groups and groups of other persuasions.

It is important to look at program variations for two reasons: (1) They

[26] Hyman and Wright, *op. cit.*, pp. 755–56. They caution, too, against studying the influence of program variables that the agency cannot modify. The evaluator's task is to identify the effects of components that are manipulable.

clarify the meaning of "the program." They fill in the details of what the general program description has outlined; they show the range of elements that are encompassed by the program-that-is. (2) They contribute to the analysis of which features of the program work and which do not. It becomes possible to look at the effects of program components and see whether some are associated with better outcomes than others. If people who are exposed to one kind of service do better than those who are not, we learn something about the relative effectiveness of different strategies and get a clue as to *why* the program is working. If some kinds of people benefit and others do not, we have further notions about the process of change. The analysis of program variables begins to explain why the program has the effects it does. When we know which aspects of the program are associated with more or less success, we have a basis for recommendations for future modifications.

Input variables

Thus, it becomes important to define and quantify the input variables. They may have to do with variations in:

1. purpose
2. principles
3. methods
4. staffing
5. persons served
6. length of service
7. location
8. size of program
9. auspices
10. management

If the program participants are seen as "put in" to the program, characteristics of participants can also be classified as input variables. Such participant measures can include:

1. age
2. sex
3. socioeconomic status
4. race
5. length of residence in community
6. attitudes toward the program (or toward health, job, marriage, movies, leisure, or whatever else is relevant)

7. motivations for participation
8. aspirations
9. expectations from the program
10. attitudes of other family members toward the program (toward health, job, marriage, and so on)
11. degree of support from family (friends, fellow workers, supervisors, and so on) for the intended goals of the program

Some of these are characteristics that the program cannot affect (age, sex), but others may change as the program goes on (aspirations, peer support). It can be important to have data on both kinds of characteristics to help define who it is that the program helps or does not help.

As evaluations of larger scope are undertaken and as national and international programs are studied, it becomes increasingly important to measure the variations among the units; that is, to measure input variables of each local Head Start, work-incentive program, concentrated employment program, Peace Corps program, and so on. Only then will it become possible to move away from blanket endorsements ("it works") and wholesale rejections ("it doesn't work") and toward the specification that it works or doesn't work under such-and-such conditions.

A note of caution is in order here. There are many variables that are interesting to study. We will even go on and talk about more. But most evaluations have limited resources, and it is far more productive to focus on a few relevant variables than to go on a wide-ranging fishing expedition.[27] Ideally, the determination of which input variables are relevant should be based on prior research, but often clear evidence is lacking. After considering the range of possible variables, the evaluator usually has to make his selection on the basis of scraps of data, the accumulated folk wisdom of practitioners, or the application of theory. Until research provides better information, these are not negligible sources of plausible hypotheses. As a rule, it will be more useful for decision purposes to study the factors the program can change ("manipulable variables," such as type of service given) than to focus on fixed attributes over which the program has little control.

Intervening variables

There can be a further phase in the measurement effort—the specification and measurement of conditions between program inputs and out-

---

[27] See Samuel A. Stouffer, "Some Observations on Study Design," *American Journal of Sociology*, LV, No. 4 (1950), 355–61.

comes.[28] The reason for giving systematic attention to these intermediate factors is the expectation that they will affect outcomes. If certain conditions obtain, outcomes will improve; if these conditions are not present, the likelihood of positive outcomes is lessened.

Program-operation variables. There are two kinds of intervening variables. One kind has to do with the implementation of the program—how the program operates. Thus, some participants in a mental health program may have one therapist throughout the program, whereas others (because of staff turnover, shifts in assignments) are served by a succession of different therapists. "Therapist continuity" is a program-operation variable that may influence the ultimate success of treatment.

Other examples of program-operation variables are: frequency of exposure (Do participants who attend 80 percent or more of program sessions do better than those with poorer attendance records?), degree of acceptance by peers (Do group members who are well-liked perform better than those with marginal group status?), extent of coordination of services (Do patients who receive all health services at one health center improve more than those who shuttle around to a number of different health facilities?). Mann offers a list of variables that can affect outcomes in behavior-change programs including the extent of opportunity for practice of new behavior patterns, degree of stress, and amount of participation of the participant and the practitioner.[29] Many factors of this sort can have consequences for the degree to which a participant benefits from the program.[30]

Bridging variables. The other kind of intervening variable has to do with the attainment of intermediate milestones. The theory of the program posits a sequence of events from input to outcome; in order to reach the desired end, certain sub-goals have to be achieved. In a rehabilitation program for prison inmates, it is assumed that learning a skilled trade will

[28] See Stake, *op. cit.,* for a somewhat different conceptualization. He speaks of, antecedents, transactions, and outcomes. His "transactions" have much in common with what we call intervening program variables.

[29] John Mann, "The Outcome of Evaluative Research," in *Changing Human Behavior* (New York: Charles Scribner's Sons, 1965), pp. 191–214.

[30] Katz, for example, discusses the importance of program variables on Negroes' intellectual performance in desegregated schools—for example, social rejection and isolation, fear of competition, and perception of threat. Irwin Katz, "Review of Evidence Relating to Effects of Desegregation on the Intellectual Performance of Negroes," *American Psychologist,* XIX, No. 6 (1964), 381–99. In more general terms, M. C. Wittrock states that it is important to measure the environment of learning and the intellectual and social processes of learners as well as their actual learning achievement. "The Evaluation of Instruction," *Evaluation Comment,* I, No. 4 (1969), 1–7.

reduce a man's chances of resorting to crime after release. Accordingly, we can measure the extent to which inmates have mastered the skill being taught in the program (as the bridging variable), and then relate skill level to the outcome measure, noncommission of crime.[31] Other bridging variables might be measured as well, such as length of time between release and getting a job, job earnings, etc., since they reflect underlying assumptions of the program. Changes in participants' attitudes or knowledge are sometimes hypothesized as necessary preconditions for change in behavior. Measures of attitude or knowledge change are then viewed as bridging variables.[32]

In sum, bridging variables are presumed to link the events of the program to the desired effects, and they represent the theory of the program. On the other hand, program-operation variables may be postulated (or discovered) as necessary conditions for the theory to operate. The two kinds of intervening variables have different implications for the planning of future programs. The bridging variable gives information about the relationship of sub-objectives to final goals. It tests the viability of underlying theory and alerts planners to modifications in assumptions or alternative theories. It might turn out, for example, that the program should be striving to reach different intermediate objectives that would be more effective links to final outcomes. The program-operation variable, on the other hand, contributes to understanding how the program has its effects, what the conditions are for effective operation. Analysis sensitizes planners to features that should be built into the program if it is to operate successfully.

Sources of intervening variables. Intervening variables are usually constructed out of the theoretical assumptions of the program. There are almost

[31] Freeman and Sherwood, *op. cit.,* give two other examples: They hypothesized improvement in reading skills as an intermediate variable on the way to reduction in school drop-outs (p. 19), and a decline in feelings of alienation and anomie as a basic step toward reduction in delinquent behavior (p. 15). Similarly, in the evaluation of in-service training I suggested a three-part analysis: Do the trainees learn the training content? If so, do they put their learning into practice? Are the trainees who practice what they have learned more successful on the job? Carol H. Weiss, "Evaluation of In-service Training," in *Targets for In-service Training* (Washington, D.C.: Joint Commission on Correctional Manpower and Training, October 1967), pp. 47–54. The extent to which immediate and intermediate goals can be divorced from ultimate goals is discussed in Edward A. Suchman, "A Model for Research and Evaluation on Rehabilitation," in *Sociology and Rehabilitation,* ed. Marvin B. Sussman (Washington, D.C.: American Sociological Association, 1965), pp. 66–67.
[32] For an analogous discussion in terms of "sub-objectives," see the report on a health service program in O. L. Deniston, I. M. Rosenstock, and V. A. Getting, "Evaluation of Program Effectiveness," *Public Health Reports,* LXXXIII, No. 4 (1968), 328–30.

always some prevailing notions, however inexplicit, that certain intermediary actions or conditions will bring about the desired outcomes. Intervening variables can also be developed empirically during the course of analysis. Although we may not have had the foresight at the outset to suspect that they were relevant, we can ask the questions of the data later, and by appropriate analysis find out whether outcomes are affected by such things as size of group, program cost per pupil, frequency of staff turnover, and so on. The only requirement is that the data must be there to be analyzed—which means the evaluator needs a modicum of cleverness or luck.

Using a model. How do we decide which variables we are going to want to measure? One way is to construct a model of the intended processes of the program. We try to identify the means and the steps by which the program is intended to work. For example, a program of home visits by teachers is inaugurated with the ultimate objective of improving children's reading achievement. How are home visits expected to improve pupil performance? We might hypothesize the sequence of events shown in Figure 3–3.

The model indicates the kinds of effects that should be investigated. Once ways are found to measure each set of events and the measurements

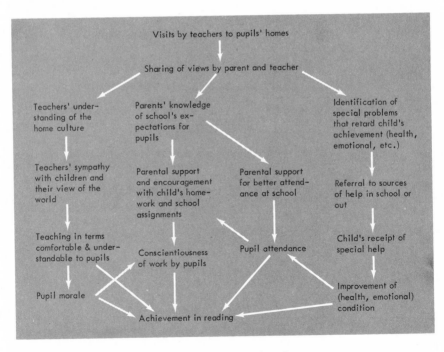

FIG. 3–3. A model of a hypothetical program.

are made, it is possible to see what happens, what works and what doesn't, for whom it works and for whom it doesn't.[33] In our home visit program, it may turn out that teachers do indeed show enhanced understanding of the culture of pupils' homes, that they have more sympathy with the children, but that they continue teaching in the old traditional ways without attempting to suit instruction to the pupils' subculture. If the children's reading performance does not improve, we have some clue about the why of it. We can tell where the projected chain has broken down. Similarly, if some parents do learn about the school's expectations for their children's behavior and performance and do try to encourage them to do better homework and schoolwork, yet their children's work is no better done than that of other children, we have a place to look for further insight into the breakdown of the expected chain of events.[34]

One of the side advantages of setting down the expected paths of change is that it sensitizes the evaluator to shifts in program strategy that make his evaluation design irrelevant. Suppose the home visit program has had difficulties in operation, and to overcome them the managers have shifted course. They have found that parents really want to talk about things other than home culture and school expectations. To maintain the parents' interest and

---

[33] As the similarity between Figure 3–3 and a path diagram suggests, path analysis is a useful way of estimating the strength of the linkages. When the necessary conditions for path analysis are met, path coefficients will represent the magnitude of effect for each arrow. See Hubert M. Blalock, Jr., *Theory Construction* (Englewood Cliffs, N.J.: Prentice-Hall, Inc., 1969).

It might be useful to posit some negative chains, too, and through path analysis find out the extent to which negative side effects are taking place.

Another analytic device, particularly useful when one step in the chain is totally or largely conditional on the one before, is the Automatic Interaction Detector (AID). Unlike path analysis, this type of "branch" analysis shows whether the program is producing strong effects for subsamples of the group. This is a matter of both theoretical and programmatic interest, because if there are differential effects, special programs can be developed to fit special groups. John A. Sonquist and James N. Morgan, *The Detection of Interaction Effects: A Report on a Computer Program for the Selection of Optimal Combinations of Explanatory Variables* (Ann Arbor, Mich.: University of Michigan Institute for Social Research, Monograph No. 35, 1964); John A. Sonquist, *Multivariate Model Building: The Validation of a Search Strategy* (Ann Arbor, Mich.: University of Michigan Institute for Social Research, 1970).

[34] An interesting analogy with the reasoning behind the construction of program process models comes from Myron Tribus, "Physical View of Cloud Seeding," *Science,* CLXIII, No. 3928 (1970), 201–10. In the complicated business of producing rain by seeding clouds, he suggests that rather than relying only on statistical measures of rainfall to evaluate success, investigators should seek to understand and measure the chain of physical events that follow cloud seeding and do or do not lead to rain.

cooperation, they have shifted to an emphasis on answering parental requests for information (about housing, health facilities, and so on). The original process model is obsolete and must be modified to reflect the new conditions. Some new processes are hypothesized and some old ones discarded; new items and directional lines are added and old ones dropped. The model is adapted to current realities, and measurements and analyses follow the new course. The evaluator, alerted early to the changes in program operations and assumptions, keeps his study flexible enough to be relevant.

The mere construction of such a model can be a useful exercise for program developers. Some of the assumptions that are implicit in the program are made explicit, and naïve and simplistic expectations are subject to scrutiny. Do program developers, for example, believe that those parents who do not have the values, the background experience, or the skills to help their children with academic studies can be persuaded to do so by one or two visits by a teacher? Certainly, more must be built into a program with such great expectations—training for the teachers, for one thing, and reinforcements, rewards, and possibly skill training for the parents. The evaluation model can be a learning tool long before the evaluation begins, if program people will use it as such.

A model is not the only way to go about the delineation of necessary measures, but it is one way to clarify and systematize the factors that are worth examining. Suppose that after home visits, pupil reading achievement improves significantly more than that of the control group students who did not have the visits. The usual conclusion would be that the visits (and all the foggy assumptions and expectations surrounding them) were justified. But suppose also that records of teachers' visits showed that all the measures of interaction, communication, and understanding between parent and teacher were at very low levels—the teachers and parents were really not communicating. The source of the children's improved reading ability must be sought elsewhere. (One explanation might be that the students misperceived the intent of the teachers' visits; they may have thought teachers were complaining about their work and trying to persuade parents to punish poor achievers. Improved school work was a response to the perceived threat.)

If the predicted sequence of events does not work out, further investigation is needed. But when the model proves to be a reasonable picture of how things happen, it gives some notion of the reasons why and may be worth further testing. Even with the best and most supportive data, of course, models are never "proved." At best, they are not "disconfirmed" by the data. There may be alternative models that would provide equally plausible or better interpretations of the available facts. Scientific generalizations are built up by developing hypotheses and then submitting them to successive tests in an effort to disprove them or find the limits of their applicability.

Collection of Data

Data for evaluation research can come from a gamut of sources and be collected by the whole arsenal of research techniques. The only limits are the ingenuity and imagination of the researcher. Some possible sources are:

1. interviews
2. questionnaires
3. observation
4. ratings (by peers, staff, experts)
5. psychometric tests of attitudes, values, personality, preferences, norms, beliefs
6. institutional records
7. government statistics
8. tests of information, interpretation, skills, application of knowledge
9. projective tests
10. situational tests presenting the respondent with simulated life situations
11. diary records
12. physical evidence
13. clinical examinations
14. financial records
15. documents (minutes of board meetings, newspaper accounts of policy actions, transcripts of trials)

Asking people

Much evaluation research relies on interviews and questionnaires to collect information about program participants—who they are, what they do in the program, and what their attitudes and behaviors are before and after program participation. Staff are frequently queried, too. Tests are a staple ingredient in the evaluation of educational programs. They provide important data on knowledge and learning. Ratings by experts are common in studies of social work, medical, and psychiatric programs.

Observation

On occasion, investigators find ways of collecting relevant data by "unobtrusive" methods that do not involve *asking* anybody anything. Thus, attendance at a science exhibit can be gauged by the number of turns of the turnstile; popularity of exhibits can be measured by the wear in the floor tiles in front of the cases or the number of requests for sample kits. People's adherence to pedestrian safety rules before and after a safety program can be measured by counting the number of people who cross against the light or outside the crosswalks. In health programs, clinical examinations and diagnostic tests have been used. For imaginative examples of these kinds of measures, take a look at Webb et al., *Unobtrusive Measures*.[35]

Observation is an important tool for collecting data on both pre- and post-program indicators and on the process itself. For maximum reliability, observations should be recorded immediately; if they lend themselves to easy classification, they can be coded on the spot.

Program records

Program records and agency files are a "natural" for evaluation data. Programs usually collect a fair amount of information about the people who participate. Whether they are pupils in a school, residents in public housing, recipients of welfare, or patients in a hospital, participants will have filled out lengthy forms giving all kinds of information about themselves and their situation. Unfortunately, experience has shown that organizational records are nowhere as useful as they should be. The organization's record keeping, the transfer of intake and service information to permanent records, tends to be haphazard. Records are inaccurate, out of date, months behind on entries. Furthermore, the definitions and categories used by the agency may be inappropriate for evaluation purposes. Vital categories of information may never have been requested, or records may be kept in a form (such as narrative case-recording) that is inordinately difficult to reduce to items usable for research.

Incompleteness plagues many agency systems. If the participants do not supply certain items of information or if the staff fails to enter data, nobody checks on the missing items and follows up. Thus, if an evaluator needs to know which college students hold outside jobs, he cannot rely on the

[35] E. J. Webb, D. T. Campbell, R. D. Schwartz, and L. B. Sechrest, *Unobtrusive Measures: Nonreactive Research in the Social Sciences* (Chicago: Rand McNally & Co., 1966).

data in the files for a complete count. Agencies sometimes change record-keeping procedures. If this happens during the period under study, it can vitiate all attempts at before-after comparisons. Just to add another horror to the gallery, there is the possibility of distortion. Agency records are often based on the reporting of practitioners, and when they know that they are being "judged" by the data in the records, they may intentionally or unintentionally bias their accounts.

On the other hand, there are compensations in the use of institutional records. One is the saving of the time and money that original data collection requires. Another is the advantage in continuity. Unlike the one-shot evaluation study that collects elegant information for a short period of time and then closes up shop, the agency reporting system can provide continual feed-in of information. As our caveats have hinted, few systems will be usable as is. The evaluator will usually have to revamp procedures, introduce new items suited to evaluation requirements, and institute checks for accuracy and completeness. If this can be done and maintained, indicators of program success are constantly on tap for on-going evaluation.

A bail bond project effectively used simple record-keeping procedures to demonstrate its worth. The program involved defendants who could not afford bail before trial. The program staff investigated to see if they had a family, home, job, or other roots in the community, and if they did, arranged to have them released from jail without bail prior to trial. In the three years that the Vera Institute of Justice ran the experiment, 3,505 persons were released. Researchers evaluated the project by looking at court records of appearance (and found that only 56 failed to appear in court).[36]

For too long, agency record keeping was relegated to a back office and a superannuated clerk. With the coming of age of computers and the change in perspective from "file cards" to data banks and information systems, institutional records have a better chance of gaining top-level attention and being upgraded. But once the new system is installed and the systems specialists have gone away, there remain a number of vital requirements if evaluation is to benefit. One is that the agency retain an evaluation capacity. Someone has to be able to analyze the products of the information system with an evaluation perspective as well as for descriptive purposes. Another is that the evaluator be in a position to bring the interpreted data to the attention of policy makers, particularly when decisions are pending for which the data are relevant. A further need is the opportunity for periodic revision of the content of the information system. Programs change; today's

[36] Herbert Sturz, "Experiments in the Criminal Justice System," *Legal Aid Briefcase* (February 1967), pp. 1–5.

emphases may be tomorrow's irrelevancies. An ossified information system quickly loses relevance to the live issues. There has to be a routine way to adapt data items and their presentation to the current scene, without at the same time disrupting items in time series that make for continuity and comparability over time. For some period, old and new items should exist side by side.

Government records

Some government agencies maintain records on individuals that would be ideal grist for the evaluator's mill. A prime example is the Social Security Administration which collects not only payroll deductions but data—on the number of quarters a person is employed, industry of employment, amount of earnings (up to the Social Security ceiling), and similar information. These data are confidential, but the Administration on occasion will release tabulations of the records of groups of people for bona fide research purposes in ways that prevent identification of individuals.[37] For evaluation of educational or job training programs, these are extremely useful follow-up data, even when gaps (such as occupations not covered by Social Security) are recognized.

School data are another good source. Depending on school regulations, information on achievement scores, attendance, promotions, and similar items can be retrieved for groups of students. Similarly, there are court records, license bureau records, motor vehicle records, and many other sources of data that are relevant for particular purposes. Automated systems are making data retrieval easier, but it is important to recognize that there are—and should be—limits on the use of records, even for legitimate research. Incursions on people's privacy is a matter of growing concern, and researchers who seek access to official records have a responsibility to limit their requests to essential items and, wherever possible, to use aggregate data (which do not identify individuals) as indicators of outcome.

Government statistical series

Another source of data for evaluation is statistical reports of other (usually governmental) agencies. Usually these data have to do with the problem that the program is supposed to "cure." Thus, if a program is designed to reduce illiteracy or highway accidents or infant mortality, the

---

[37] For example, Bernard Levenson and Mary S. McDill, "Vocational Graduates in Auto Mechanics: A Follow-up Study of Negro and White Youth," *Phylon*, XXVII, No. 4 (1966), 347–57.

evaluator can turn to statistical reports on the prevalence of these ills and look at changes in the statistics from a time before the program starts periodically through to some later period. If the program is effective, presumably it will tend to push the figures down. Of course, it is necessary that the program and the indicators be coterminous, that they cover the same geographic area. If the program is working to reduce illiteracy in one neighborhood of St. Louis, it is hardly fair to judge its success by studying the statistics on illiteracy for the whole city.

Scope. Evaluation on the basis of changes in existing indicators is still more a dream than a reality. At the present time there are only limited social data available, and these not necessarily on the most important issues. Much of the data is collected locally, and definitions and categories—even meanings—vary from city to city. Very few data are available for small areas, such as the neighborhood, at which most programs still work.

Accuracy. Furthermore, accuracy is a sometime thing. Crime statistics, for example, have been found to be riddled with reporting peculiarities. There have been at least two newsworthy instances when a new chief of police took office, improved the record-keeping system—and was confronted with a big jump in the crime rate. Victimization studies, surveys that ask representative samples of the public about their experiences as victims of crime, show that large numbers of crimes are never reported to the police. Many statistical series reflect administrative actions as well as the "pure" incidence of the problem. Delinquency rates reflect the activity of the police in apprehending juveniles as well as the actual rate of juvenile crime. Rates of the incidence of diseases depend on the health department's case finding as well as on the existence of the cases.

Definition of terms. Definitions of terms may also fail to accord with the evaluator's needs. Standard unemployment figures do not include the underemployed, people who are working part-time but want full-time employment, nor do they count people out of work who have gotten discouraged and are no longer actively looking for a job. Recent Labor Department surveys have found that in poverty neighborhoods, unemployment rates can be substantially understated because of these omissions. If an evaluator wants to use these figures to judge the success of a program for reducing hard-core unemployment, neither the before nor the after figures are suited for his purpose.

Separating effects. In recent years, there has been a movement to develop a national system of social indicators. The proposed system would solve many of the current problems—increase the scope of data, institute common definitions and categories so that data can be compared from place to place, improve accuracy, and certainly allow for disaggregation of data on a small-area basis. There are persuasive reasons for moving toward better social accounting. But as Sheldon and Freeman note,[38] even much better social indicators will not solve all the evaluator's problems. For evaluation purposes, there is no way of separating out the effects of the program from all the other factors operating on the indicators. If the illiteracy rate goes down, it is not necessarily true that the program was solely, or even mainly, responsible.

Geographic base. Another problem is that indicators are generally based on geography rather than on people. They include any people who are living in the area at a specific time. In some areas, particularly in urban poverty neighborhoods, residents are highly mobile. The people who lived there and were served in the program last year are no longer around to show up in this year's indicators. It is a whole new batch of people whose status is being measured. If higher-income people have moved into the neighborhood, the changes in the indicators may look exceedingly favorable, even though the real target group is not better off—only farther off.

The fact that indicators cover areas, and thus populations larger than the service scope of the program, minimizes a program's capacity to make a dent in the numbers. A city will have figures on the percentage of people who vote city-wide and in each precinct, but not figures on voting for the people who were exposed to a get-out-the-vote campaign. It would require changes of heroic proportions in the exposed group to shift the city-wide or precinct percentages of voters.

Inexactness. There is a temptation in using indicators to make do with the figures that exist, even if they are not direct measures of program goals. The use of surrogate measures, or what Etzioni calls "fractional measurement," is common in all social research, since one indicator rarely captures the entire concept in which we are interested.[39] It is probably particularly likely in evaluation-by-social-indicator because of the limited supply of appropriate indicators. For example, we may have a program to improve the quality of housing in an urban neighborhood. There are no available figures on housing quality, but there is a figure on overcrowding, that is, the number of persons per room. The evaluator makes a series of assumptions leading to the conclusion that overcrowding is a reasonable indicator of housing quality, and then draws conclusions about the success of the program on the basis of a measure that at best is only a partial indicator of the true objective.

[38] Eleanor B. Sheldon and Howard E. Freeman, "Notes on Social Indicators: Promises and Potential," *Policy Sciences,* I (1970), 97–111.
[39] Etzioni and Lehman, *op. cit.,* p. 2.

Manipulation. Indicators are also susceptible to manipulation. Once national indicators are established, program personnel—like the teacher who teaches to the test—may work to improve those facets of their operation that they know will show up and be judged, and pay less attention to changing the complex social conditions that indicators only partially reflect. [40]

Expectations. Perhaps the gravest impediment to the use of social indicators for evaluation is that it expects so much. A program must be *pervasive* enough to reach a significant part of the relevant population and *effective* enough to bring about change sufficient to shift people from one category to another. A little bit of change is not enough; people have to move from "hospitalized" to "not hospitalized," from "below grade level" to "on grade level," from "unemployed" to "employed." This is asking for program success of giant magnitude. Programs generally reach relatively small numbers of participants and make small improvements. Even the poverty program, considered to be a massive undertaking at the time, was able to mobilize resources that were scanty in comparison with the size of the problem. It is little wonder that indicators resist dramatic change.

Even if change does come, it is apt to take a while to show up. Indicators are sluggish. They are derived from periodic soundings, usually annual, so that there is a considerable time lapse before trends become apparent. By the time changes appear in the figures, numbers of other influences have been operating on conditions, and we are back to the problem of authenticating the program as the source of effects.

Some reasonable uses. Nevertheless, there are conditions under which the use of indicators for evaluation would make eminent sense. For massive programs, such as public education or Medicare, they can provide time-series data on the distribution of resources and outcomes.[41] They would have the advantage for federal decision purposes of using common criteria and collecting comparable data across projects and across time, and if astutely constructed, dealing in issues of relevance to policy makers. They cannot overcome such inherent limitations as the failure to account for external (nonprogram) influences or the absence of information on causes and dynamics of change. But if supplemented by, and related to, specifically evaluative studies on critical issues, their information on nation-wide conditions could be supportive and important.

[40] Campbell, "Reforms as Experiments," pp. 409–29.

[41] Cohen, *op. cit.,* pp. 234–36, proposes a system of social indicators of schools and schooling that would permit analysis of inputs to schools, outcomes of schooling, and "temporal, geographic, political and demographic variation in both categories."

4

Design of the Evaluation

Once the evaluator knows *what* he is going to study, the next step is to decide how to study it. He develops a plan to select the people to be studied, set the timing of the investigation, and establish procedures for the collection of data. In developing his design, he can aim for the traditional controlled experiment or for one of the less formalized quasi-experimental designs. He can restrict his investigation to one project or look at the outcomes of a number of projects with the same basic goals. He can deal in the traditional social science variables or he can proceed to an economic analysis of the program's costs and the benefits it produces. These options are the subject of the present chapter.

Experimental Design

The classic design for evaluations has been—in exhortation if less often in practice—the experimental model. This model uses experimental and control groups. Out of the target population, units (people, work teams, precincts, classrooms, cities) are randomly chosen to be in either the group that gets the program or the "control group" that does not. Measures are taken of the relevant criterion variable (for example, factory work-group productivity) before the program starts and after it ends.[1] Differences are computed, and the program is deemed a success if the experimental group has improved more than the control group. Figure 4–1 illustrates the model graphically.

	Before	After	
Experimental	a	b	If the difference between a and b is greater than the difference between c and d, the program is a success.
Control	c	d	

FIG. 4–1.   An illustration of an experimental model.

The control group does not necessarily receive *no* program. That is a fruitful comparison only if the decision to be made is a choice between this program and none at all. Often, the choice will be between the experimental program and the usual treatment for the group, such as the standard factory supervisory practices. The control group in this case receives the standard treatment. In cases where no real treatment can be offered to controls, a "placebo" program can be devised that gives the aura, but not the substance, of service. It removes the possibility of a "Hawthorne effect," a positive response that is due merely to the attention that participants receive.[2] Avoiding Hawthorne effects is an important

[1] Actually "before" measures are not a necessary condition for an experiment. If the randomization is trustworthy, after measures alone will suffice. The before-and-after usage provides a check on the adequacy of the random assignment and is particularly useful if numbers are small (and sampling error might cause initial differences between the two groups even with randomization). Also with before-and-after measures, statistical computations are likely to be easier. Further, individuals who changed can be analyzed separately during the data analysis to learn something about how they differ from those who did not change. On the other hand, "before" measures may sensitize subjects to the measurement instrument and cause a change in scores due solely to the effect of retesting. To guard against this contingency, there can be two control groups, one of which is pretested and one which is not.

[2] The term comes from a series of studies made at the Hawthorne Works of the Western Electric Company between 1927 and 1932. Researchers found that when management paid attention to workers, no matter what shape it took, output increased. For example, decreasing illumination, as well as increasing it, led to higher output. Although recent re-examination of the data has thrown some doubt on the interpretation in this case, the "Hawthorne effect" is a phenomenon that has been observed in many situations.

consideration, but it appears unwise for both ethical reasons and those of public policy to provide a service to controls that is patently phony, like the sugar pill of pharmacological experiments. The alternate service should have some likelihood of doing good. One possibility is offering controls a cheap version of the program under study. Thus Scriven suggests that controls in a curriculum project might receive a quickie curriculum developed over a summer by graduate students.[3] This can be viewed as a placebo, but it might turn out to be as effective as the master curriculum painstakingly developed by specialists.

Randomized designs are a very effective way to rule out the possibility that something other than the program is causing improvements that are observed. After all, people do mature with time and might conceivably change on their own. For example, somewhere about the age of seventeen or eighteen, young men generally become less likely to commit crimes and more likely to hold jobs—a phenomenon that has confounded evaluators of delinquency prevention programs whose research lacked control groups. They were tempted to attribute these good results to the program under study. Outside events also have an effect on people. They are exposed to a multiplicity of influences, from changes in the economy and the availability of jobs to changing emphases on television shows. The controlled experiment effectively rules out the contention that it was this outside "history" that brought about the observed changes. It protects against other sources of invalid conclusion-jumping, too.

Campbell and Stanley list eight major threats to internal validity, that is, eight classes of outside (non-program) variables that can affect the outcomes of an experiment if they go uncontrolled. We have mentioned maturation and history. Others are: testing, the effects of taking a test upon the scores of a second testing; instrumentation, changes in the calibration of measuring instruments or changes in the observers or scorers; statistical regression, which operates when groups have been selected on the basis of their extreme scores and on a second testing tend to move back toward the mean score of the group; selection, choosing experimental and control units with different characteristics; experimental mortality, differential loss of respondents from experimental and control groups; selection-maturation interaction, the differential maturation of members of experimental and control groups.[4] Randomization protects against all these sources of possible confusion in analyzing results.

[3] Michael Scriven, "The Methodology of Evaluation," in *Perspectives of Curriculum Evaluation,* ed. R. W. Tyler, R. M. Gagné, and M. Scriven (Chicago: Rand McNally & Co., 1967), p. 69.

[4] Donald T. Campbell and Julian C. Stanley, "Experimental and Quasi-Experimental Designs for Research on Teaching," in *Handbook of Research on Teaching,*

Some problems

The controlled experiment, however, is often impossible in action settings. There may be absolutely no "extra" people to serve as controls; the program serves everybody eligible and interested.[5] Even if there are unserved people, program practitioners may refuse to assign any of them to a control condition because they believe it is their professional obligation not to "deny service." [6] Occasionally, the only possible controls are widely scattered, far away, or unlikely to cooperate with a program that offers them nothing in return.

The randomized assignment procedure of the experiment also creates problems. Practitioners generally want to assign people to "treatments" on the basis of their professional knowledge and experience. They want to decide who can most benefit from service and which kind of service is most suitable, and not leave the process to chance. Furthermore, even when randomized assignment has been achieved, participants may drop out during the course of the program, a factor over which the evaluator has no control. The remnants of either the experimental or the control group, or both, may be unrepresentative of the original groups in important and unknown ways. Experiments are particularly vulnerable to Hawthorne effects. With all the conspicuous machinery of randomization, participants are likely to be unduly aware of their specialness. Controls may be aggrieved, angry, perhaps relieved, but in some way affected by their rejection by the program.

On occasion, control groups become contaminated because the members associate with people in the program and learn what they have been doing. Sometimes other agencies come along and provide the "controls" with the same kinds of services that program participants are receiving. Or, as Rossi notes, a changing economic or political climate can make

---

ed. N. L. Gage (Chicago: Rand McNally & Co., 1963), p. 175. Reprinted as *Experimental and Quasi-Experimental Designs for Research* (Chicago: Rand McNally & Co., 1966).

[5] A program that had difficulty in getting enough referrals is reported in H. J. Meyer and E. F. Borgatta, *An Experiment in Mental Patient Rehabilitation* (New York: Russell Sage Foundation, 1959).

[6] See Edgar Borgatta, "Research: Pure and Applied," *Group Psychotherapy,* VIII, No. 3 (1955), 263–77, for an excellent discussion of practitioners' objections to control groups and researchers' replies. The objection that withholding service is unethical is countered by the contention that if the treatment is of no value, it is wasteful to give it.

services available to the presumably sheltered controls which are equivalent in many respects to the program being studied.[7]

This is a sad litany. But imaginative evaluators have made a number of ingenious adaptations. In the Stanford Computer Assisted Instruction program, the half of the group receiving CAI *reading* instruction was the control for the half receiving CAI *math* instruction, and vice versa.[8] In the evaluation of a medical school program, Kendall arranged to have half the class receive the new program during the first semester and the other half during the second semester.[9] She took measures at three points—before the program began, at the end of the first semester, and at the end of the year. For the first-semester group, the then-unexposed second group provided controls; for the second-semester group, the first group (even though they were now unequal) were the controls. In effect, the experiment was repeated twice. (See Figure 4-2.) Moreover, the third measure, taken a full semester after the first group had been exposed to the program, gave evidence of whether effects persisted or faded away over time. This type of staging, or delayed treatment, would appear to have wide applicability.[10]

In the last few years, the experimental model has come under attack not only because it is not feasible, but because it is counterproductive. Guba and Stufflebeam, for example, fault the experimental model because:

1. It requires holding the program constant rather than facilitating its continual improvement.
2. It is useful for making decisions only after a project has run full cycle and not during its planning and implementation.

[7] Peter H. Rossi, "Boobytraps and Pitfalls in the Evaluation of Social Action Programs," *Proceedings of the Social Statistics Section* (Washington, D.C.: American Statistical Association, 1966), pp. 127–32.
Not all these problems are unique to the experiment. Some, such as the contamination of control groups and the differential attrition of experimentals and controls, can also occur in other designs, such as the quasi-experimental designs discussed in the next section.

[8] Edward L. McDill, Mary S. McDill, and J. Timothy Sprehe, *Strategies for Success in Compensatory Education: An Appraisal of Evaluation Research* (Baltimore, Md.: The Johns Hopkins Press, 1969).

[9] Patricia Kendall, "Evaluating an Experimental Program in Medical Education," in *Innovations in Education,* ed. Matthew B. Miles (New York: Teachers College Bureau of Publications, 1964), pp. 343–60. In this study, students were not randomly assigned to the two groups, but the technique can clearly be used with randomization.

[10] An interesting example of staging in a psychotherapy program is described in Carl R. Rogers and Rosalind F. Dymond, *Psychotherapy and Personality Change* (Chicago: University of Chicago Press, 1954), esp. pp. 38–47.

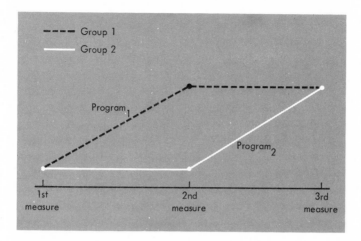

FIG. 4–2.   Expectations for effects of program on two "staged" groups.

3. It tries to control too many conditions, making the program so aseptic that it is ungeneralizable to the real world.[11]

In view of the way evaluations are being done, these criticisms have point and weight. But none of them is an inevitable concomitant of the controlled experiment. The experimental method does not require a stable program. It can be used even when the program meanders. If there is interest in the effects of a program under developmental conditions or in its usual nonstandardized form, randomized designs are perfectly suitable for studying outcomes. If the question is a comparison between the original "model" program and a naturally evolving version of it, it is possible to divide the program into two subunits, one of which remains stable and the other of which is encouraged "to improve continually" on the basis of best opinion. Or the basic principles of the program can be established and maintained, while variations in operation are described and classified after the fact. (We will talk more about the changing program and how to cope with it in Chapter 5.)

Outcome results can be compared at regular intervals—monthly, quarterly, or whatever. There is no need to wait until the program has completed its full cycle if usable indicators of at least intermediate success

[11] Egon G. Guba and Daniel L. Stufflebeam, "Evaluation: The Process of Stimulating, Aiding, and Abetting Insightful Action," address delivered at Second National Symposium for Professors of Educational Research, November 21, 1968. (Columbus, Ohio: Evaluation Center, College of Education, Ohio State University.)

are possible to come by. With shorter subcycles, it is also possible to allow for a greater number of variations (changes) in treatment. Each participant can be assigned randomly to each treatment; with such a crossover design, the results of different program components become available. Or different subgroups can be exposed to different treatments and the results measured. With interim measures and shorter subcycles, evaluation results can be reported back to guide managers during the conduct of the program. Successive modifications of the program are in turn evaluated. Further, if several units of a program can be run simultaneously or seriatim, all kinds and varieties of "contamination" and "interference" can be studied.

Experimental techniques need not be applied unimaginatively by the book, although they often have been. Too many studies have been done on a one-project, one-time basis, taking little advantage of the benefits of comparative study, repeated periodic measurement, and sophisticated design and analysis. Wiser use of available methodology would certainly enhance the usefulness of experiments.

Use of experimental design

The basic issue is one of fitting the research design to the purpose of the study. Experimental design is an elegant way to find out how well a particular program achieves its goals. If that is the issue, the experiment is the optimal design. If the program manager wants to know something else entirely—what the needs are in the area, how to develop a new program, how to secure acceptance, or how to set up and implement the program —he should look to other kinds of applied research, rather than evaluation. If he wants information for day-to-day management purposes, a good automated record system, supplemented by periodic follow-up measures of outcome, is likely to be the most help. If he wants "formative" information on program effectiveness, he may need only rough estimates, and these on the real program as it shifts and changes. In this case, simpler techniques—cheaper, faster, easier to manage, and less demanding of program staff—can serve the purpose.[12]

The purpose of the evaluation study, the use to which results will be put, should determine the study design.[13] It is for purposes outside the immediate program that experimental design is best suited. Decisions on

[12] Egon G. Guba, "The Failure of Educational Evaluation," *Educational Technology*, IX, No. 5 (1969), 29–38.

[13] See Edward A. Suchman, "Action for What? A Critique of Evaluative Research," in *The Organization, Management, and Tactics of Social Research*, ed. Richard O'Toole (Cambridge, Mass.: Schenkman Publishing Co., 1970).

the order of continuation or abandonment of the program, decisions on whether to advocate nation-wide use of the program model—these require great confidence in the validity of the research, and therefore experimental design. Other types of decisions may not need such rigor, at least initially. Rossi suggests that a first go-round with "soft" techniques (correlational, ex-post-facto, one-group before-and-after) can show whether a program warrants further evaluation. Only if the reconnaissance phase detects positive effects is it worthwhile going on to a controlled experiment.[14]

The essential requirement for the true experiment is the randomized assignment of people to programs. Experimentalists suggest that this is much more possible in the real world than many of us suspect.[15] When resources are scarce and some people must do without, randomization is possible; when new programs are introduced over a period of time, the delayed receivers can become the controls for those who get the programs early; special pilot projects can be designed on an experimental basis. But however possible the conditions may be—and more power to those who can bring them off—experience suggests that they do not often obtain. Programs are rarely run for the convenience of the evaluator, and his requirements are only occasionally a factor in the program (and funding) arrangements. In these circumstances, the trend toward quasi-experimental design is a hopeful sign.

Quasi-experimental Designs

Quasi-experimental designs, designs that do not satisfy the strict requirements of the experiment, have been given a boost toward legitimacy by the work of Campbell and Stanley.[16] Their influential paper (later reprinted as a monograph) catalogues preexperimental, experimental, and quasi-experimental designs of varying degrees of satisfactoriness. The basic criterion for how satisfactory they are is the extent to which they protect against the effects of extraneous variables on the outcome measures. The best designs are those that control relevant outside effects and lead to valid inferences about the effects of the program. Unlike experimental design, which protects against just about all possible threats to internal validity, quasi-experimental designs generally leave one or several of them uncontrolled.

Quasi-experiments have the advantage of being practical when condi-

[14] Rossi, *op. cit.*, pp. 127–32.
[15] Donald T. Campbell, "Reforms as Experiments," *American Psychologist*, XXIV, No. 4 (1969), 409–29.
[16] Campbell and Stanley, *op. cit.*, pp. 171–246.

tions prevent true experimentation. But they are in no sense just sloppy experiments. They have a form and logic of their own. Recognizing in advance what they do and do not control for, and the misinterpretations of results that are possible, allows the evaluator to draw conclusions carefully. Quasi-experiments, in their terms, require the same rigor as do experimental designs.

Time-series design

The time-series design is one of the most attractive quasi-experiments. It involves a series of measurements at periodic intervals before the program begins and continuing measurements after the program ends. It thus becomes possible to see whether the measures immediately before and after the program are a continuation of earlier patterns or whether they mark a decisive change. For example, Figure 4–3 shows three cases in which be-

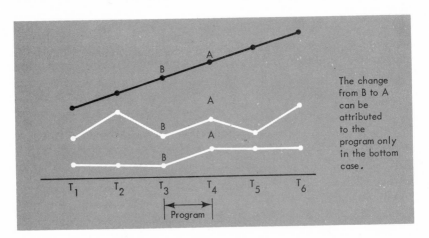

FIG. 4–3.   Examples of three time series.

fore (B) and after (A) measures will have different significance. The time series probably protects against all threats to validity except history. Some special events might have come along at the same time as the program and led to the observed effects.

Multiple time series

Even better is the multiple time-series design. If the evaluator can find a similar group or institution and take periodic measurements of it over the same time span, he can protect against the confounding effects of history as well. This design appears particularly appropriate to evaluations of school programs, since repeated testing goes on normally and long series of pre- and post-scores are often available.

An interesting example of multiple time series was the evaluation of the Connecticut crackdown on highway speeding. Evaluators collected reports of traffic fatalities for several periods before and after the new program went into effect. They found that fatalities went down after the crackdown, but since the series had had an unstable up-and-down pattern for many years, it was not certain that the drop was due to the program. They then compared the statistics with time-series data from four neighboring states where there had been no changes in traffic enforcement. Those states registered no equivalent drop in fatalities. The comparison lent credence to the conclusion that the crackdown had had some effect.[17]

Nonequivalent control group

Another design is the nonequivalent control group. Here there is no random assignment to program and control as there would be in a true experiment, but available individuals or intact groups (classrooms, hospital wards) with similar characteristics are used as controls. Nonrandomized controls are generally referred to as "comparison groups." Before and after measures are made for both groups and results are compared. This design obviously has to contend with selection as a possible source of misinterpretation—as well as the interaction of selection with other factors and possibly, if groups were selected for extreme scores, regression effects.

The nonequivalent control design is probably the most common design in practice. A major issue is how to make the comparison group as similar to the experimental group as possible. Matching procedures are sometimes resorted to—pairing up members of the experimental group and controls on available measures, or matching the whole experimental group to a similar group at the start of the program. Afterward, when one group has been exposed to the benefits of the program and the other group has not, the difference between them should be due to the program. But matching is much less satisfactory than randomized assignment on several counts. Not the least is that we often cannot define the characteristics on which people should be matched. That is, we don't know which characteristics will affect whether the person benefits from the program or not. We may have matched on age, sex, race, and IQ, when the important factor is

[17] Campbell, "Reforms as Experiments," pp. 418–19.

motivation. As some wit has said, if we knew the key characteristics for matching, we wouldn't need the study.

Matching is sometimes done on the basis of pretest scores. If the measures are not highly reliable, this tends to be a poor procedure. (Note that we are talking about matching without randomization. If units are matched and then randomly assigned to each group, the procedure increases the statistical precision of the experiment. Matching as a prelude to randomization may even be essential when there are few units, such as cities. But matching as a substitute for randomization can produce pseudo-effects.) It can produce particularly misleading results when experimentals and controls are drawn from basically different populations. Regression effects get in the way of valid interpretation. Regression is not intuitively obvious, but the simple case is easy to understand. All measures contain some component of "error," and some, such as test scores and attitude measures, contain a sizable amount. On any one testing, some individuals will score artificially high and others artificially low; on a second testing, their scores are likely to be closer to the mean. If participants and "controls" are chosen on the basis of their extreme scores, they are likely to regress toward the mean, with or without the program. At a second testing, what look like effects of the program may be artifacts of statistical regression. For example, see Figure 4–4, a case in which there are no program effects. It is better in dealing with nonequivalent controls to compare the measures of natural groups than to select only extreme cases by matching. In Figure 4–4, this would mean using the E_1 and C_1 measures rather than E_2 and C_2.

Self-selection is another thorny problem in selecting a comparison group. People who choose to enter a program are likely to be different from those who do not, and the prior differences (in interest, aspiration, values, initiative) make post-program comparisons between "served" and "unserved" groups risky. Cain and Stromsdorfer found a comparison group for unemployed workers in a job training program from lists of unemployed persons who would have been eligible for the program but had not had contact with it.[18] Main used unemployed friends of job trainees for comparison.[19] In both cases, however, checking disclosed that the groups were not comparable in several respects.

The search for controls who are as like program participants as possible has led to the use of "unawares" (people who did not hear of the program,

[18] Glen Cain and Ernst W. Stromsdorfer, "An Economic Evaluation of Government Retraining Programs in West Virginia," in *Retraining the Unemployed,* ed. Gerald Somers (Madison, Wis.: University of Wisconsin Press, 1968), pp. 299–335.

[19] Earl D. Main, "A Nationwide Evaluation of M.D.T.A. Institutional Job Training," *Journal of Human Resources,* III, No. 2 (1968), 159–70.

but might have joined had they heard) and "geographic ineligibles" (people with characteristics similar to participants, but who lived in locations that had no program). Each ingenious stratagem solves some problems and raises others. What was there about the unawares that blocked their knowledge of the program? What are the effects of community conditions in the different location? The question has been raised whether it is important to eliminate self-selection bias in program evaluation. Since voluntary programs

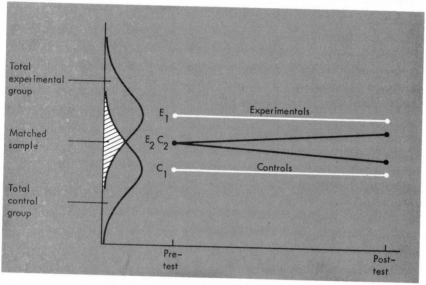

FIG. 4–4. Regression artifacts in a matched sample.

inevitably include self-selected participants, would it perhaps be appropriate to evaluate the combined effects of self-selection and program participation? Such a procedure would certainly simplify the control group problem and the evaluator's life, but study results would have to be interpreted with considerable caution. Although it is possible to think of cases where those most in need of service enter a program, it is usually the better risks who select themselves in. If they show better outcomes than the controls, a plausible explanation is that they would have prospered whether there was a program or not.

Self-selection problems can sometimes be overcome if both experimentals and controls are selected from volunteers. (If the volunteers are randomly assigned to either group, we have the conditions for a true experiment.) An interesting variation was used in a New Jersey court study of pretrial conference, a procedure in which the judge summons litigants to a conference before the trial to try to settle the case. Pretrial conference was obligatory at that time in state courts, but the question arose whether it actually helped to settle cases. For legal reasons, the court was unwilling to deny pretrial to any group of litigants. It did, however, agree to make pretrial optional; half of the cases would be pretried only if one of the litigants demanded it. This enabled the researchers to compare the obligatory pretrial with the optional pretrial group (about half of whom chose to forgo it). Since cases were randomly assigned to the two groups, they were even able to conduct a true experiment.[20]

Even when randomized assignment is not feasible, it is usually better to have a nonequivalent comparison group than no controls at all. We are better off being able to rule out some possible explanations for observed effects than not rule out any. Sometimes it is possible to locate natural groups (students in another college, employees in a different department) to use for comparison purposes. The more similar they are in their recruitment and the more similar their answers on the pretest measures, the more effective they will be as controls. What differences exist between them and program participants should be measured and reported, and the evaluator should indicate the direction of bias stemming from noncomparability, noting whether it tends to understate or overstate program effects.

Patched-up design

Probably the most engaging and cogent feature of the quasi-experimental approach is the realization that it is not essential to guard against every possible source of error. The aim should be to control those sources of error likely to appear in a given situation. Thus, Campbell and Stanley include a design specifically dubbed "patched up," because it adds specific controls, one after the other, to rule out different sources of confusion.

> As a part of this strategy, the experimenter must be alert to the rival interpretations (other than the effect of X [the program]) which the design leaves open and must look for analyses of the data, or feasible extensions of the data, which will rule these out.[21]

[20] Hans Zeisel, "Reducing the Hazards of Human Experiments through Modifications in Research Design," *Annals of the New York Academy of Sciences,* Vol. 169 (1970), 475–86.

[21] Donald T. Campbell and Julian C. Stanley, *op. cit.,* p. 227.

Although not neat and elegant, such designs solve important problems in the real world.

Advantages of quasi-experimental designs

The aim to identify plausible interpretations that rival the program as the source of change and to rule *these* out is a familiar type of inference in nonresearch situations. Thus, if Tommy is standing in the middle of the room with fragments of a broken vase at his feet, we are not impressed with the need to rule out the possibilities that the wind blew over the vase or that it cracked spontaneously. The one rival hypothesis we will investigate is that Barbara pushed Tommy while he was holding the vase, since she is standing behind him, and he is yelling "Barbara made me." There are often plausible explanations for results showing *no change,* other than failure of the program. These deserve systematic attention, too.

While experimental design has prestige, power, and symmetry, quasi-experimental design often has the overriding virtue of feasibility. The evaluator who attempts a controlled experiment, encounters obstacles, and fouls up is less productive than the one who adapts his designs—in line with good research practice—to the possibilities. Quasi-experimental designs can produce results that are sufficiently convincing for many practical purposes.[22]

Nonexperimental Designs

On occasion, it is impossible to use even quasi-experimental designs. The evaluator, unless he retires from the lists, has to resort to one of the three common nonexperimental designs: before-and-after study of a single program, after-only study of program participants, or after-only study of participants and non-random "controls." Their inherent weakness is that they fail to control for many of the rival explanations (that observed changes were caused by something other than the program).

At their best, they can be full of detail and imagery, provocative, and rich in insight. If the data are collected with care and system, they offer more

---

[22] For suggested applications of quasi-experimental designs to the field of socio-legal research, see Richard Lempert, "Strategies of Research Design in the Legal Impact Study: The Control of Plausible Rival Hypotheses," *Law and Society Review,* I, No. 1 (1966), 111–32.

information than would have been available without any study at all. For "formative" purposes, this may well be adequate. But for "summative" purposes, they are much less satisfactory than more rigorous designs. At worst, the data they produce are misleading. In all cases, they leave considerable room for differing interpretations of how much change has occurred and how much of the observed change was due to the operation of the program. But with all the caveats, there are times when—failing other alternatives—they may be worth considering.

First, they can provide a preliminary look at the effectiveness of a program. If, for example, before-and-after study (with all the contaminating effects of outside events, maturation, testing, and so on) finds little change in participants, then the program is probably having little effect. It may not be worthwhile to invest in more rigorous evaluation. This kind of preliminary reconnaisance may be particularly apt for evaluation because: (1) experience shows that many programs produce little gain, and (2) most of the contaminating factors artificially elevate the level of gain. Thus, a finding of little success with a design that tends to enhance the illusion of success is important information. (Note, however, that program effects may be *underestimated* if special outside events operate to counteract program efforts, or if participants are compared with "controls" who can be expected to do better—say, because of higher socioeconomic status or higher ability.) If change does appear, the program can be subjected to further study under experimental conditions to determine how much of the change is attributable to the program.

A second reason for considering nonexperimental designs arises from current federal practices for funding evaluations of major social programs. Many government agencies tend to demand one-time ex post facto investigation; they are responding to political pressures and short-term needs, and they want quick results. The system of competitive contracting for evaluation leaves the major decisions in their hands. The way the system works is that the agency develops a "request for proposal" (RFP) for evaluation of its program. The RFP specifies the purpose, scope, design, and time schedule for the study. Research organizations are invited to submit applications to undertake the work as specified in the RFP, and after review, one applicant organization is selected. The evaluator thus has the choice of either refusing to enter the game (which is sometimes the better option) or accepting the RFP specifications. Until federal agencies show wider recognition of the fallibilities of the ex post facto approach, much important evaluation will continue to be done on this basis, and evaluators will have to exploit every opportunity to supplement and expand the basically inadequate design.

Other circumstances, too, restrict the evaluator's options—he may not be called in until the program is in midstream, he may not have access to comparison groups. Since a great deal of evaluation is still being done under restrictive conditions, it seems useful to consider whether there are ways to overcome any of the basic flaws.

One-project before-and-after

This type of evaluation need not be limited only to pretest and posttest measures. It can take a series of measures of participants as they move through the program and see how well they attain the sequential steps that have been hypothesized. This follows the logic of the program process model described in Chapter 3 (refer again to Figure 3–3). Data of this kind can be supplemented by intensive qualitative analysis of the events of the program in an attempt to understand the relationships between program services and participant progress. If the agency is interested in information on its effectiveness in *delivering* services (that is, in its outputs as well as its outcomes), the evaluation can study the processes of program implementation and find out the extent to which the program is producing the quantity, quality, and coverage of service that were expected.[23] These data can then be related to participant outcomes. Although results from a single case study are not readily generalizable to other programs, they can provide insights that will help the program improve its operations.

After-only

In the ex post facto design, the pickings are even leaner. Knowing how program recipients are faring after service has meaning only if there is good reason to expect what their condition would be without service. This is not often the case. Although there may be clues from past experience or from earlier research, they rarely take into account all the current contingencies. The first thing the evaluator can do is collect retrospective reports from participants on their status prior to the program, thus providing a pseudo-pretest measure. Retrospective self-reports are not always reliable, particularly on attitudinal measures; people often distort their reports on the past, usually in the direction of congruence with present attitudes. But on

[23] Herman D. Stein, George H. Hougham, and Serapio R. Zalba, "Assessing Social Agency Effectiveness: A Goal Model," *Welfare in Review*, VI, No. 2 (1968), 13–18.

"hard" items, such as age, number of years of schooling, whether they were employed or unemployed, the responses are probably fairly trustworthy. It is sometimes possible to find records that contain reliable preprogram data on participants—for example, applications for entrance to the program, hospital records, housing records. In addition, the evaluator can ask about participants' experiences in the program (although such data also have limitations) in order to permit analysis of the effects of particular kinds of experiences. If at the time of the evaluation there are people in various stages of the program—some just entering, others part-way through, others nearing the end—data can be collected on their status on the outcome measures. Provided that recruitment procedures have not changed and that there has not been a high rate of drop-out during the program, comparisons with program "graduates" on these measures can give some indications of program effectiveness. (This type of comparison, in effect, moves us to the next design: after-only with comparison groups. Because there is little risk of differences in selection, this is a fairly strong comparison.) Whatever the elaboration, the design remains vulnerable to many confounding effects (history, maturation, selective drop-outs, the particularities of program implementation), and the evaluator has to determine how relevant such factors are likely to be.

After-only with comparison group

The after-only design can be strengthened by adding a comparison group which is as similar to program recipients as possible. Some studies have used next-door neighbors of participants, residents of the same neighborhoods, students in the same schools. They can be interviewed on the same set of antecedent, process, and outcome items. When records are available on relevant items for the before and after periods (welfare status, school achievement, days of absence from work), these will be eminently useful. Sometimes data for similar groups can be retrieved from national or local surveys. For example, if the program serves black urban males, it may be possible to get tabulations of data for the subsample of black urban males from surveys of employment, health, voting, and so on.[24] However,

[24] Underhill reports on a national pilot survey of poor youth undertaken specifically to determine the feasibility of such data to serve as "controls" for the evaluation of antipoverty programs for this age group. He collected indicators on background, experience, ability, self-concept, and attitudes. Ralph Underhill, *Methods in the Evaluation of Programs for Poor Youth* (Chicago: National Opinion Research Center, June 1968).

it takes a good bit of luck to find data that are relevant, complete, and accurate enough, and measures that are reliable and stable enough, to serve the evalutor's purposes.

Whatever devices are used, the comparison group will almost inevitably differ from the participant group in important ways; the sheer fact that participants selected themselves into the program is a persuasive indication. Without the pretest data that are available in the quasi-experimental "nonequivalent control group" design, although perhaps with makeshift pretest data, it is especially difficult to disentangle the prior differences from the effects of program service. Sometimes statistical procedures (usually analysis of covariance) are used to try to "equate" program and comparison groups, but this has generated considerable controversy. Critics contend that it chronically *underadjusts* and thus leaves an uninterpretable composite of selection differences and program effects.[25] Defenders of the procedure claim that whatever underadjustment there may be is usually puny in comparison with the massive effects, or more often the massive no effects, of the program.[26] All the evidence is not yet in, but under some circumstances, there is reason to be wary.

The best course is to extend data collection and move to quasi-experimental design. Starting with his posttest measures of one group, the evaluator can take similar measures of new groups entering the program; the posttests of the first group can be compared with pretests of the next group; pretests of this group can be compared with their posttests. In this iterative fashion, more valid conclusions can be drawn. Similarly, additional measurements can be "patched on" to test whatever other rival hypotheses challenge the validity of evaluative conclusions. For ongoing programs, there is great value in instituting a continuing data system that includes information on participant characteristics, program services, and outcomes

[25] Donald T. Campbell and Albert Erlebacher, "How Regression Artifacts in Quasi-Experimental Evaluations Can Mistakenly Make Compensatory Education Look Harmful," in *Compensatory Education: A National Debate,* Vol. 3 of *The Disadvantaged Child,* ed. J. Hellmuth (New York: Brunner and Mazel, 1970), 185–210.

[26] Victor G. Cicirelli, "The Relevance of the Regression Artifact Problem to the Westinghouse-Ohio Evaluation of Head Start: A Reply to Campbell and Erlebacher," *op. cit.,* pp. 211–15; John W. Evans and Jeffrey Schiller, "How Preoccupation with Possible Regression Artifacts Can Lead to a Faulty Strategy for the Evaluation of Social Action Programs: A Reply to Campbell and Erlebacher," *op. cit.,* pp. 216–20; Donald T. Campbell and Albert Erlebacher, "Reply to the Replies," *op. cit.,* pp. 221–25; John W. Evans, "Head Start: Comments on the Criticisms," in *Britannica Review of American Education,* Vol. 1, ed. David G. Hays (Chicago: Encyclopedia Britannica, Inc., 1969), 253–60.

(including some long-term follow-up measures). Many programs are not discrete entities but ongoing activities, and such time-series data provide an effective basis for continuous stocktaking and program modification.

Comparative Evaluation
of Programs

Most evaluations are done one program at a time. Study of a single program can show whether participants are better off after the program than they were before. If control groups are used, the evaluation can discover whether it was the program that brought about the benefits rather than extraneous outside conditions. If the controls, instead of receiving no service, receive the ordinary type of program (regular classroom, regular ward), the results of the study indicate whether the new program is superior to the old.

But sometimes this is not all that decision makers want to know. They need information on the comparative benefits of different kinds of programs. For example, in the job training field, they want to know the relative advantages of residential training centers, neighborhood training and placement programs, and on-the-job training. In many areas where old remedies have failed, the search is not for a program that is slightly better than nothing or than the past; it is for the best among a whole series of innovative and experimental ideas being tried. Evaluation research can be designed to compare the effectiveness of several programs that have the same objectives but different content on the same set of outcome measures.

Even within a single program, there are significant possibilities for comparative study. Many national programs are carried out through a series of local projects, with local variations in strategy and procedure. Cross-program study—that is, evaluation of all or a sample of the local projects—can yield information on the relative success of different methods of program implementation for the attainment of the common goals.

Even the study of a number of projects that are presumably doing the same thing (for example, using nonprofessionals as teacher aides) can turn up important findings. Some projects may be using the aides for routine classroom chores, like taking attendance; others may be using the aides for tutoring individuals or small groups of students in elementary skills; still others may be relying on them as interpreters and intermediaries between the culture of the children and the culture of the school. A cross-program study that is alert to these differences in function can increase the value of evaluation of teacher aide programs.

The increase of information is of two kinds—increase in generalizability of results, and increase in the specification of which strategy under which conditions has better effects with different kinds of participants.

Generalizability

The single project is the prisoner of its setting. The evaluation is confined to observing effects in one time and place, with a particular staff and target group in a specific agency, under the conditions of the moment. It is often hard to know how far the observed results can be generalized to other situations.

All too often, too, the personality of the innovator and the excitement of the experiment create conditions that maximize effectiveness. An innovating teacher develops a curriculum and teaches it with such enthusiasm that students make remarkable progress. But the same curriculum, when turned over to routine teaching and regular teachers, fizzles. The initial results are never reproduced. If cross-program evaluation were done, the special case would not stand out and mislead.

Let us imagine fifty child health centers, all with the same objective of improving the health of low-income preschool children. If we study them together, we can average the results and get an overall indication of program effects. This will wash out any unique factors that elevate or depress outcomes in one or two locations. For example, if one center happens to have a uniquely dedicated staff and therefore obtains outstanding results, these extreme results will not be given the undue weight that would accrue to them if *only* this center were evaluated. They will be stirred into the pot with forty-nine other centers' outcomes, and more representative "average" figures of outcome will show. The results will be more typical and thus more generalizable to child health centers at large—that is, they will have greater external validity.

Specification

On the other hand, comparative study allows us to precipitate out of the common pot those program characteristics that influence results. The evaluator need not content himself with overall averages. He can compare programs with different inputs, and analyze the outcomes of centers with some particular characteristic against those of other centers. This enables him to see whether the feature is associated with better or poorer outcomes. Thus, the fourteen centers in locations accessible by public transportation may turn out to serve a much higher percentage of their potential client group than the thirty-six centers not so accessibly located. The ability to isolate factors that "work" is a major contribution of cross-program evaluation.

On a cross-program basis, experimental design (with its requirement of randomization) is almost never feasible. There is some hope that in the future Congress will appropriate funds specifically for experimental testing of new program ideas, but even this hope is romantic. At present in the hurly-burly of program life, a good multiprogram quasi-experiment would mark a big step forward.

In its most advanced form, comparative cross-program study will be based on theoretical assumptions about the nature of people's needs and the kinds of help that programs offer. Thus a program of vocational training for high school drop-outs might have three patterns worth testing, each based on somewhat variant theories about why traditional programs have not worked in the past. The first pattern is a three-component program— basic education, skill training, and counseling. It is based on the "deficit" supposition—that drop-outs are deficient in education and training and that personal counseling can motivate the individual to benefit from the opportunities offered. The second program is the male model variant. The belief here is that the drop-out's key need is for effective male figures with whom to identify. Therefore, while offering the same three components, it uses dynamic and able male teachers. The other variant is the community hookup project, which sees the problem in the lack of visible coordination between school courses and the real world of work. Thus, while also giving the same program, its distinguishing feature is skill training in an actual on-the-job setting.

Each of these project variations is introduced into a number of communities, preferably of different types—large and small, urban and rural, North and South. Trainees are recruited into each program by the same procedures. Then the evaluator observes the effects of each. Let us say he chooses as an indicator of program success the percentage of trainees earning at least X dollars weekly three months after the conclusion of training. He collects the data and fills in the cells of Figure 4–5. He can now compare the effectiveness of each program type both *overall* and in each kind of community. He has the basis for quite specific recommendations on which program type is most likely to be successful in communities with different characteristics. By further analytic elaboration—for example, classifying types of trainees (male/female, under 21/21–45/over 45)—he can make his conclusions increasingly specific. If he has enough cases to study, he can deal with a number of variables at a time.

Comparative study of this type has great power. But programs are rarely set up with conscious and orderly variations for the researcher to study. Nor does he usually have the authority or the influence to institute conditions conducive to good design. If he is lucky and clever, he can capitalize on variations that occur naturally. Thus, in studying one hundred community action agencies, Vanecko found that agencies could be classified by their primary goals into three groups—those that emphasized educational and social service goals, those with community organization goals, and those with employment goals. His analysis looked at program activities and effects in terms of this three-way classification.[27]

Community Type	Program Type		
	Standard	Male Model	Community Hookup
A			
B			
C			
D			
All Communities			

FIG. 4–5. An illustration of comparative research in a vocational training program.

Many government programs, like the community action program, are not so much unitary programs as a congeries of diverse efforts addressed to the same problem and funded from the same pot. Within the program there are different emphases and different strategies. If the evaluator studies a large number of community mental health centers or Head Start or Peace Corps or employment programs, he can probably identify a few different

[27] James J. Vanecko, "National Evaluation of Urban Community Action Programs," Report No. 1, National Opinion Research Center, University of Chicago, June 1969; *idem,* "Community Action Program Goals for Institutional Change: Preliminary Report on National Evaluation of Urban Community Action Programs" (Chicago: Center for Urban Studies, University of Illinois, July 1969); James J. Vanecko with Susan R. Orden and Sidney Hollander, "Community Organization Efforts, Political and Institutional Change, and the Diffusion of Change Produced by Community Action Programs," NORC Report No. 122 (Chicago: National Opinion Research Center, April 1970); Office of Economic Opportunity, *Reports from the 100-City CAP Evaluation* (Washington, D.C.: OEO, 1970).

types of theories that provide the bases for action. He can categorize them and the program activities along a number of significant dimensions, and then relate the type of program to outcomes. In that way, although the design is not elegant, he can make some headway toward specification of what works and does not work under given conditions.

Some problems, some advantages

The problems, of course, remain legion. Because projects are not assigned randomly to communities and clients are not assigned randomly to program types, there are bound to be all kinds of uncontrolled, even unidentified, sources of variation. To name just a few, results will be affected by local conditions, by recruitment strategies (some programs selecting the neediest and some selecting those most likely to succeed), by differences in community support, staff capability, program stability, and interactions among these. Perhaps some of the factors can be identified and measured, and their effects analyzed, but it will be an enormous task, and methodological purists will certainly throw up their hands. Results will inevitably contain more uncontrolled variation than researchers like to deal with, and the interpretation of results will never be precise.

Even when distinct "program strategies" are established or identified, it is often difficult to see that they are maintained. A recent study of the Follow Through program in the early grades of elementary school began as a quasi-experimental examination of the relative effects of different program strategies. School district participation in the study was voluntary, thus ruling out in advance the advantages of random selection of schools. Each school district selected its own strategy from among a number of models. Even then, the evaluators found the school districts reluctant to maintain the program strategy intact if there seemed better ways to help students learn. They wanted evaluation to feed back information on how to improve the program, not wait until a long period had passed and then render judgment: "Your model was right, but *your* model was wrong." They disliked the horse-race competition of comparative evaluation, the feeling of being pitted against each other. Instead of vying with one another, they felt that they should be cooperating to learn to do the task better.

This is an illustration on a large-scale basis of cross-purposes for evaluation. The evaluators wanted to find out how well different programs work ("summative" evaluation), while the school people wanted to know something else—how to make the program work better ("formative" evaluation). Unless purposes are clear, comparative multiproject evaluation—like all other evaluation—founders on discrepancies in expectations.

The tale also highlights problems of shifting programs, program "designs" that don't stay put but that purposely or inadvertently change focus and direction. The next chapter discusses this problem further.

Furthermore, the case history illustrates a pervasive political problem. Federal policy makers may contract for cross-program evaluation to provide information for their decisions, but effective control of programs (even when they are funded from the federal purse) often rests with local managers. The federal agency rarely has the authority to impose conditions necessary for rigorous evaluation. In the case of the Follow Through program, the most serious limitations were the inability of many schools to administer the program with sufficient intensity to make a difference in what went on in the classroom (obviously a crucial factor), together with midstream shifts in program strategy and, in some cases, in basic program goals as well. Some communities moved away from the goal of improving school achievement, which was to be the common indicator of program effectiveness, toward goals of parent or community control of schools.[28] As we have noted before, evaluation falls heir to the problems that afflict programs— in this case, decentralization of power and discrepancies in priorities between federal and local decision makers.

We started this discussion of comparative evaluation with high enthusiasm for the knowledge that accrues from comparative study, but practical difficulties seem to have intruded and dimmed our expectations. We should note, too, that cross-program study requires large sums of money and a high order of research management skills. Despite these obstacles, it retains the potential for making important contributions to our understanding of social programming. Experience suggests that it is worth the effort and expense particularly under three conditions:

1. When the issues are real, when policy makers are faced with vital decisions among alternative strategies of action.
2. When the alternative programs are relatively well-defined, with substantially similar aims but clearly differentiated strategies for attaining them. (Each alternative program may have some goals the others do not share, but they should have a set of core goals in common.)
3. When there is evidence that the programs have the viability and strength to offer some likelihood of success. Embarking on the demanding course of comparative evaluation appears foolhardy for weak, low-intensity, or untried programs. Comparative evaluation should probably be a second-stage effort after earlier study shows the probability of some positive outcome.

[28] David K. Cohen, "Politics and Research: Evaluation of Social Action Programs in Education," *Review of Educational Research*, XL, No. 2 (1970), 213–38.

Until planners are convinced of the utility of basing decisions on research evidence, the existence of conditions necessary for good cross-program study will probably be a fortuitous occurrence. In the meantime, the best functional substitutes are two: a grounding in theory and replication.

Theory and Replication

One of the most important elements in producing a useful evaluation is locating the study in a theoretical perspective. Programs are expected to work because they meet needs, affect processes, set events in motion. Our vocational training program, for example, supplied male teachers for boys to identify with, or hooked up with jobs in actual plants. There has to be some reason—some theoretical justification—to expect a program to succeed. In Chapter 3 we discussed this grounding in theory in terms of the process by which effects take place and outcomes are produced. As we make assumptions explicit and test the linkages from step to step, we begin to accumulate knowledge that is usable and transferable to a variety of program settings. It is in probing the theoretical premises of the program that evaluation can ultimately become most practical.

The other essential is replication, now a relative rarity in evaluation research. Not often does a second investigator study the effects of the same type of program using the same criteria of success. It looks like unexciting and pedestrian work. Yet repeated investigation is vital for confidence in the validity of evaluation results. As the noted statistician R. A. Fisher said, the standard of firm knowledge is not one extremely significant result, but repeated results of statistical significance. Repetition of results is the basis of scientific generalization. And through repeated investigation, we can increasingly specify the conditions under which programs succeed or fail and the processes by which success and failure come about.

Cost-Benefit Analysis

Cost-benefit analysis is often viewed as an alternative to evaluation research. But essentially it is a logical extension of it. In order to affix dollar values to the benefits of a program, first there has to be some evaluative evidence of what kinds and how much benefit there has been.

Much cost-benefit analysis has been done in a prospective framework, assessing the likely costs and benefits of alternative strategies being proposed for the future to reach a given end (for example, to reduce infant mortality). The emphasis has been on planning—widening the range of options, estimating what each option will cost in terms of the returns it will bring, and introducing rational analysis into the decision-making process. But much cost-benefit analysis has also been applied retrospectively to calculate the returns on investment in past programs. It is this use that meshes most closely with evaluation, although there is obviously an evaluative cast even to prospective analysis. For untried programs, data—both on costs and benefits—are likely to be more sparse, but the same considerations apply.

In essence, the cost-benefit analyst attempts to identify the benefits of a program, both tangible and intangible; he looks at the costs of conducting the program, the direct and indirect; then he tries to put them into a common unit of measure—dollars. The ratio of benefits to costs is an indication of the return that society is getting from its investment in the program.

In identifying the benefits that accrue from a program, the cost-benefit analyst is in the same boat as every other evaluator. He is concerned with appropriate indicators of outcome, control or comparison groups, intervals for stock-taking (right after the program? two years later?), collection of valid data, and so on. However, because determination of outcomes is only one aspect of the job, and because cost-benefit analysts generally come from disciplines that do not specialize in original data collection, he is likely to rely on available records, statistical series, or other sources at hand, and make the extrapolations or adjustments that seem necessary. A good evaluation study of the program under consideration (or even of similar ventures) would be a big asset for he could then proceed more readily to the quantification of benefits and costs.

Quantifying benefits

The intangible benefits of a program are particularly hard to quantify. How much is it worth to society for program participants to have heightened feelings of self-esteem or less anxiety about paying future medical bills, or to keep a family from dissolution? Some analysts have given up trying to calculate the monetary value of intangibles like these and limited their attention to tangible returns. But Dorfman calls this a case of "horse-and-rabbit stew": The rabbit is the small proportion of effects that are susceptible to measurement, while the flavor of the stew is dominated by the "horse" of social, psychological, and esthetic considerations that defy measurement.[29] Cost-benefit analysts have to cope with this problem by

[29] Robert Dorfman, ed., *Measuring Benefits of Government Investments* (Washington, D.C.: The Brookings Institution, 1965), p. 2.

acute selection of indicators of benefit, and by qualitative reporting of factors not succeptible to monetary expression.

Traditionally the dominant concern of cost-benefit analysis has been the level of national income; a program that increases total income is deemed a good investment. But most programs involve both gains and losses. Thus a significant issue is the *distribution* of costs and benefits. Who is getting the benefits and who is paying the costs? It turns out that often different segments of the population are involved; for example, taxpayers are paying the costs, and farmers, or unemployed workers, or owners of private airplanes receive the benefits. The distributional effects, and their relative values, are not reflected in total dollar calculations, but they may be vital for policy making.[30] Is it a greater benefit to redistribute social goods to one social group than another? The use of a system of weights has been proposed, reflecting the relative values of gains for specific groups but it is not clear how such weights could be developed. One thing that can be done is to report outcomes for different groups separately. Or if a program is specifically designed to aid a particular group, the benefits to them can be calculated and compared with the costs (forgone consumption to the rest of society.[31]

The factors to be included in the calculation of benefits remain a subject of dispute. What should be considered, for example, in computing the benefits from the cure of a drug addict? Should you calculate the increase in his probable lifetime earnings, or these *plus* the costs saved to society for welfare payments, hospital treatment, police enforcement, incarceration in prison, injury to probable victims, and so on? Differences in assumptions result in cost-benefit conclusions for the same program that differ by orders of magnitude.

What numerical quantities should be assigned to the benefits? The analyst's general procedure is to estimate what a public good would "sell for" if it were sold on the private market. Thus, in estimating the dollar benefit of a prevented death (say, from a traffic safety program), he might look at jury awards for deaths in court suits. But there is often little consensus on any given set of figures. One way out of the morass is to posit a fixed level of benefits and assume that alternative programs are all designed to reach the same goal. Under this fixed-benefit strategy, the analyst looks at the costs that different programs incur to achieve the given level of benefit; the least expensive one is the best bet. Another bypass of the quantification problem is to report outcomes in their "natural dimension," for

---

[30] Thomas K. Glennan, Jr., *Evaluating Federal Manpower Programs: Notes and Observations* (Santa Monica, Calif.: The RAND Corporation, September 1969), pp. 12–14.

[31] *Ibid.*, p. 14.

example, number of days in hospital, number of households displaced from neighborhoods where they lived for more than two years.[32] The decision maker can consider the information and assign his own weights in arriving at policy choices. Clearly, the measurement problem is far from solved.

There are theoretical issues involved, too. To move from evidence of outcomes to dollar benefits, analysts often posit causal theories of amazing grandeur. As Rivlin notes, recent translations of achievement test scores in grade school into increases in lifetime earnings make heroic assumptions: that raising a child's achievement level by a full grade in a short period has the same implications for future earnings as the completion of another grade in school; that test score gains will not erode with the passage of time; that the value of additional time spent in school can be inferred from census data on the average earnings of people with differing years of schooling.[33] The last assumption may be particularly suspect, since there is ample evidence that years of schooling and earnings are both related to the antecedent factor of family social class. To ascribe earnings solely to schooling (and inferential schooling at that) ignores the importance of social class background on both variables. When cost-benefit analysis rests on dubious theory, it is an uneasy guide indeed.

Technical considerations

Cost-benefit analysts have to cope with a variety of technical considerations as well. For example, the choice of an appropriate discount rate for future benefits is a matter of some debate. To oversimplify the issue, consider a dollar spent today that provides a return of two dollars twenty years from now. Most of us would shy away from the investment; putting today's dollar in the bank at 5 percent interest will give a greater return, not to mention the possibilities of more productive investment. The discount rate is a way to take into account the cost of forgone opportunities (for investment, for current use). It reduces future benefits by some percentage to compensate for the alternatives that have been given up. The use of different discount rates can significantly affect cost-benefit results.

In some cases, a marginal as well as an average cost-benefit ratio is called for. When an existing program is expanded, the same cost does not necessarily provide the same benefits—for example, when the expanded

[32] Jerome Rothenberg, "Cost-Benefit Analysis: A Methodological Exposition," paper presented at American Academy of Arts and Sciences Conference on Evaluation of Social Action Programs, May 1969 (Cambridge, Mass.: Massachusetts Institute of Technology, 1969), pp. 28–29.

[33] Alice M. Rivlin, *Systematic Thinking for Social Action* (Washington, D.C.: The Brookings Institution, 1971), p. 55.

program reaches deeper into the ranks of the disadvantaged or necessitates recruitment of less qualified staff. The analyst must calculate the cost-benefit ratio for the incremental investment.

Cost-benefit analysis is most used and most useful in these cases: (1) when existing data (or easily collectible or credibly reconstructible data) indicate the scope and degree of program impact; (2) when the main benefits can be reduced to dollar terms without overly fancy guesswork or neglect of crucial effects; and, at least up to now, (3) when general benefit level rather than distributional change of benefits is the main criterion. Analysts have proved remarkably ingenious even when these conditions do not apply, and work is going on in a number of fields to standardize assumptions and adopt common conventions in order to improve the comparability of analysis. But as successive studies introduce refinements in technique, the vulnerability of the conclusions to changes in assumption becomes clear.

An allure of this type of analysis is that it moves evaluation conclusions from the realm of interesting description into the value system and terminology that make sense to many policy makers. There is something so cogent and attention-getting about cost-benefit calculations (possibly too cogent, given the current state of the art) that those who ignore them almost seem to court inefficiency. Particularly when alternative programs are being considered to achieve substantially similar ends, they rationalize and simplify the process of choice. Even for dissimilar programs, by introducing comparable information regarding return on social investment, they clarify the issue of value: *What is the policy maker willing to pay (or forgo) to achieve a given kind and level of benefit?*

This, it seems to me, is the right question to pose, and cost-benefit analysis should be cheered on in its efforts to improve the quality of its data. Such analysis cannot supersede or sidestep the political decision-making process by reducing the matter of choice simply to a game of numbers. Even if we knew that benefit-cost ratios were higher for one type of program than another, we would not necessarily choose the program yielding the higher return. The decision would depend in large part on the values we attach to the goals. But it does introduce elements of clarity, comparability, and simplification into complex situations and in so doing, helps policy makers express their value preferences more accurately.

From Evaluation to Planning, Programming, and Budgeting

If evaluation and cost-benefit analysis are to have an effect on decisions, there has to be some way to move from the data to the decision—some system for transmitting information and feeding it into the decision process. The Planning-Programming-Budgeting System (PPBS) recently in use in the federal government is such a system. But it starts at the other end, with the definition of government objectives.

PPBS was introduced into the Department of Defense under Secretary McNamara in 1961, and it proved so successful that in 1965 President Johnson instructed all federal departments to install the system. There is little new in the individual concepts of PPBS, but in combination they provide a systematic approach to governmental planning. The distinctive characteristics of PPBS are these:

1. It identifies and defines the fundamental objectives of the government and considers all activities (regardless of which department conducts them) in relation to those objectives.

2. It explicitly and systematically identifies alternative ways of carrying out the objectives.

3. It estimates the total cost implications of each alternative, including capital and noncapital costs, direct and support costs. It looks not only at the coming year, but several years into the future.

4. It estimates the expected benefits of each alternative. There is some advantage to reducing benefits to dollar terms, but qualitative information can also be used.

5. It presents the resulting cost and benefit comparisons for each alternative, along with identification of major assumptions and uncertainties. Thus, it helps executives and legislators to base decisions on the widest scope, best data, and most sophisticated analysis available.[34]

PPBS has been primarily concerned with future options rather than past experience. But in estimating expected benefits, it has to derive its figures from somewhere. This is where evaluation should come in.[35] Let us take a

---

[34] For a good collection of readings, see *Planning Programming Budgeting: A Systems Approach to Management,* eds. Fremont J. Lyden and Ernest G. Miller (Chicago: Markham Publishing Co., 1968). A short description of PPBS appears in *What is PPB? Planning Programming Budgeting for City State County Objectives* (Washington, D.C.: State-Local Finances Project of the George Washington University, 1967).

[35] Some observers see a sharp difference in perspective between PPB and evaluation. The prospective focus of PPB is associated with innovation and the confident expansion of federal activity; evaluation is retrospective, suitable to a time of disillusionment with past initiatives, stock-taking, and retrenchment. Allen Schick, "From Analysis to Evaluation," *Annals of the American Academy of Political and Social Science,* Vol. 394 (1971), 57–71. These differences in political climate may be an accident of history. It seems possible that evaluation, too, can provide the springboard for innovation and expansion, based on better informed analysis of strategies for successful programming.

hypothetical case. Under the objective of providing for public safety, a city is considering four programs: an increase in police foot patrols, improved street lighting, a new jail, and preventive group work with youngsters in high-crime neighborhoods. If evaluation research has been done—in this city or even in other similar jurisdictions—the analyst can use the results to compare the benefits (and costs) likely to accrue from each approach.

The very process of analysis forces people to think about the objectives of government activity—what they want to achieve—and to consider choices explicitly, with benefits and costs in mind. If alternative programs can be designed to reach the same ends, PPBS highlights the comparisons and enables decision makers to bring all the available information to bear.[36]

But one of the major limitations on effective use of PPBS is the dearth of good information. Without evaluative evidence, the whole procedure becomes a series of guesses. Joseph Wholey, reporting on the first attempt to apply PPBS to maternal and child health programs in the Department of Health, Education and Welfare, makes the point a little more gracefully:

> Little information was available, either through routine reporting or through program evaluation studies, on the degree to which existing federally supported maternal and child health programs (individually and collectively) reduced number of chronic handicapping conditions, reduced infant mortality rates, or reduced unmet dental needs. . . . As a result of the lack of data on effectiveness of existing maternal and child health programs, decisions on possible expansion of these programs were bound to depend almost entirely on "professional judgment." [37]

Without data, the successive exercises of Planning-Programming-Budgeting become a yearly spinning of wheels. Partly because program effectiveness data—evaluation—have not improved noticeably in either coverage or quality, much of the enthusiasm has gone out of the PPBS movement. In addition, it became obvious that only a limited number of alternatives could be analyzed in a given period so that much decision making and budgeting continued to be done on an incremental basis (rather than starting with the presumed clean slate), and that entrenched programs with well-organized constituencies were highly resistant to dramatic modification.[38] There

[36] See William Gorham, "Notes of a Practitioner," *The Public Interest*, No. 8 (Summer 1967), 4–8; Elizabeth B. Drew, "HEW Grapples with PPBS," *The Public Interest*, No. 8 (Summer 1967), 9–29.

[37] Joseph S. Wholey, "The Absence of Program Evaluation as an Obstacle to Effective Public Expenditure Policy: A Case Study of Child Health Care Programs," in *The Analysis and Evaluation of Public Expenditures: The PPB System*, A Compendium of Papers Submitted to the Subcommittee on Economy in Government of the Joint Economic Committee, 91 Congress, 1 session, Vol. 1 (1969), 451–71.

[38] Charles L. Schultze, *The Politics and Economics of Public Spending* (Washington, D.C.: The Brookings Institution, 1968), pp. 77–92.

were operational problems, too. Drags in the system included the tie-in to the budget process with its own traditions and fixed routines, limited analytic capability in many departments, and the heavy costs that PPB entailed. But the lack of a good information base was basic.

In July 1971 the federal government dismantled much of the PPB apparatus, although features of the system survive in a number of departments. Ways are being sought to accomplish similar planning objectives without the old elaborate format. Even in retreat, PPB has left some notable legacies not the least of which is heightened interest in better program information and data systems. PPB has been adopted in a number of state, county, and city governments, and is being considered in others. When better evidence of program benefits is collected through evaluation research, PPB, or some variant of it, remains a potential method for linking evaluative data to the decision-making process.

5

The Turbulent Setting
of the Action Program

A characteristic of evaluation research that differentiates it from most other kinds of research is that it takes place in an action setting. Something else besides research is going on; there is a program serving people. In fact, the service program is the more important element on the scene. The research is an appendage, an also-present, a matter of secondary priority. Researchers frequently propose changing the order of priority, and with some justification. If we do not find out whether the program is really doing what it is supposed to be doing, how do we know whether it is worth having at all? But whatever the cogency of the argument in any particular circumstance, the program almost universally remains the first order of business. The evaluation has to adapt itself to the program environment and disrupt operations as little as possible.

Obviously, some interference will take place. For one thing, data have to be collected. Staff members and program participants will be asked questions, observed, asked to fill out forms. Certain research requirements are uncompromisable. But all too often, evaluators ask for more information than they need or will ever use. With a clear focus for the study and some self-restraint, they can lower their demands and lessen their intrusion. But however cooperative and congenial the evaluator may be, there are some features of an action setting that can create serious research problems. We will discuss three in this chapter: (1) the tendency of the program to change while it is being evaluated, (2) the relationships between evaluators and program personnel, and (3) the fact that the program is embedded in an organizational system and that the nature of the system will have consequences for outcomes.

The Shifting Program

In an earlier chapter we anguished over the complexity of social programs and recommended serious attention to monitoring, describing, and classifying program characteristics. The conscientious evaluator, heeding this advice, completes his specification of the program and files it away. Then in midstream, while the evaluation is still going on, the program slithers out of his carefully constructed categories. Conditions change and the program changes.

It may change little by little, as practitioners see that present methods are not working and conscientiously innovate until they find satisfactory arrangements. Perhaps changes in clientele or in community conditions lead to subtle changes in activities and principles. Or the program may change quite suddenly. More money becomes available—or less. Staff members resign, and staff with different viewpoints or qualifications are hired. The political winds shift, and old relationships are shut off. A decision is made in Washington or the state capital to discontinue certain styles of operation and adopt others. Such factors affect even programs set up as "demonstrations," "models," or "social experiments." The longer and more complex the program, the more likely it is to experience change. For the evaluator even to know that the program is changing requires periodic stock-taking. He has to be in close enough touch to talk to directors and staff, examine records, perhaps attend meetings or observe the program in session. One signal that should alert him to turn up on the scene is a change in top program management.

If the program has altered course, what does the evaluator do? If he goes ahead as if he were studying the same program, he will never know what it was that led to observed effects or the lack of them—the old program, the new one, the transition, or some combination of everything going on. If he drops the original evaluation and tries to start over again under the changed circumstances, he may lack appropriate baseline data. He may not have measures relevant to the new goals and program procedures.[1] Further, he has no guarantee that the same kind of shift will not occur again.

One thing he can do is update his original specification of the program through continuing observation and definition. He can develop a dynamic rather than a static model of the program to categorize it in terms of its movement as well as its conceptual location. This makes for a more complex description of what the program is, but one more in touch with reality.[2] That, you may think, is all very nice; we are certainly for program descriptions that are dynamic and accurate over those that are static and wrong. But in evaluation, we usually want to learn which component, which strategy, of the program is associated with success. How does even an accurate dynamic description help us here?

The issue for the evaluator

The way that the issue is frequently posed: How can we hold the program steady? The assumption is that when things are changing, there is no way of separating out the useful components from those that are neutral or counterproductive. Continuity of input seems essential for any fair test of what the effects of that input are likely to be. Observers have proposed a variety of solutions. Some authors, and Fairweather is a good example,[3] recommend that when innovative programs are being tested, the researcher should be in control of the entire operation. Then the program will be conducted with evaluation requirements in the forefront and random changes will be fended off. Even when the researcher is not in control, he can still play the role of advocate for program maintenance. Freeman and Sherwood suggest that the evaluator has the responsibility to hold the program to its original concepts and principles. He should stand over it "like a snarling watchdog" to prevent program practitioners from altering its operations.[4]

Mann, after reviewing several hundred evaluations, found that pro-

---

[1] Sidney H. Aronson and Clarence C. Sherwood, "Researcher Versus Practitioner: Problems in Social Action Research," *Social Work,* XII, No. 4 (1967), 89–96.

[2] See Alfred P. Parsell, "Dynamic Evaluation: The Systems Approach to Action Research," SP–2423 (Santa Monica, Calif.: Systems Development Corporation, 1966).

[3] George W. Fairweather, *Methods for Experimental Social Innovation* (New York: John Wiley & Sons, Inc., 1967), pp. 24–36.

[4] Howard E. Freeman and Clarence C. Sherwood, "Research in Large-scale Intervention Programs," *Journal of Social Issues,* XXI, No. 1 (1965), 11–28.

grams are too complex and variable in operation to provide fair tests of program principles. For drawing conclusions about the relative merits of different approaches, he gives up on action settings and recommends taking programs back to the laboratory. There small segments of program can be studied rigorously, and successful practices can be identified for given conditons. Once this type of basic knowledge is obtained, the individual components can be built back up into operable programs.[5] Weiss and Rein have looked at large-scale programs that are exploratory and unclear in orientation, that inevitably cast about for new directions and methods. In cases such as community-action or model-cities programs, they believe that it is better to discard the investigation of goal achievement altogether. The researcher will learn more from careful analysis of what is actually going on. He can investigate such pressing issues as why and how programs change, how agencies absorb new inputs of money and direction and emerge relatively unscathed, how adaptations are worked out between innovative programs and resistant systems.[6]

Perhaps it is possible to redefine the controversy. Holding the program steady, let alone controlling it, is beyond the authority of most evaluators in most settings I have seen. There *are* programs that remain clear, coherent, and intact by themselves without the evaluator's cajolery or imprecations. But if they are under strong pressures to change, there is a limit to what he can do to hold back the tide. On the other hand, surrender to complexity and retreat to the laboratory look like a cop-out. It is true that many programs are rushed into the field prematurely without the painstaking developmental work required for effective service. We are in a hurry for solutions; we want to serve thousands of people right away. Although the program may be inadequately conceptualized, we hope that the whole thing will somehow work and that at our leisure, we can sort out the features responsible for the success. It is worth heeding Mann's advice that more research should be directed toward the careful development and testing of program components. Furthermore, for the accumulation of a body of tested knowledge about the relative effectiveness of strategies, a grab-bag collection of disparate evaluations is hardly the ideal basis.

But the laboratory is not the real world. In the artificiality of the laboratory, all manner of things seem to work that do not survive their brush with operating conditions. Even optimum program components will get contaminated when they emerge, and further research will have to be done under

[5] John Mann, "The Outcome of Evaluative Research," in *Changing Human Behavior* (New York: Charles Scribner's Sons, 1965), pp. 191–214.

[6] Robert S. Weiss and Martin Rein, "The Evaluation of Broad-Aim Programs: A Cautionary Case and a Moral," *Annals of the American Academy of Political and Social Science*, Vol. 385 (September 1969), 118–32.

an almost limitless set of circumstances to define the "best" components for each contaminated condition.

Some practical approaches

To cope with such problems, Suchman has proposed a four-stage developmental process.[7] He differentiates a pilot phase, when program development proceeds on a trial-and-error basis; a model phase, when a defined program strategy is run under controlled conditions; a prototype phase, when the model program is subjected to realistic operating conditions; and an institutionalized phase, when the program is an ongoing part of the organization. It is only in the model phase that the program must be held stable for experimental evaluation. At other stages, less rigorous study suffices, and variation in input is not only tolerated but expected. If an agency were committed to such a rational course of development (and maintained it!), it would effectively resolve the issue of program shifts. The evaluator may find it rewarding to encourage the agency to move toward such clear demarcation of program phases, with appropriate evaluation at each step.

The approach that Weiss and Rein propose is, I think, refreshingly relevant for programs of the scale and ambiguity that they discuss, although they give only fragmentary clues to the methods by which such complex processes can be analyzed. What they recommend is basically a study of the implementation process, rather than evaluation. We know that implementation is a critical juncture between the best-laid plans of program developers and the "gang aft agley" of operation.[8] The differences in perspective between

----

[7] Edward A. Suchman, "Action for What? A Critique of Evaluative Research," in *The Organization, Management, and Tactics of Social Research*, ed. Richard O'Toole (Cambridge, Mass.: Schenkman Publishing Co., 1970).

[8] In defining the career of social problems, Herbert Blumer lists five stages, the fifth of which is "the transformation of the official plan in its empirical implementation." He goes on to say, "Invariably to some degree, the plan as put into practice is modified, twisted and reshaped, and takes on unforeseen accretions." "Social Problems as Collective Behavior," *Social Problems*, XVIII, No. 3 (1971), 301, 304–5. For a description of federal planners' "naïveté" about the complexity of translating official plans into operating programs, see Walter Williams, "Developing an Evaluation Strategy for a Social Action Agency," *Journal of Human Resources*, IV, No. 4 (1969), 451–65. He notes three aspects that impinge on implementation: How well articulated the plan is, how administratively capable the local staff is, how much authority the federal agency has to force compliance (or obversely, how much political insulation the local agency has to resist change).

planners and operators, the pressures that beset the local program, the responses necessary for survival and support all alter and reshape the original concept. Understanding what happens in the political and social complexities of broad-aim intervention programs may well be a priority order of business if we are to learn how to develop programs more realistically, to reduce the slippage between intent and action, and to address social problems with greater effect. Present inattention to this facet of program life is difficult to understand or condone.

Nevertheless, study of implementation does not supplant evaluation of outcomes. Critical as it is to learn more about the dynamics of operation, it remains important to find out the effects of the resulting programs on people and institutions. The two research efforts should be complementary. As we learn more about implementation, we can begin to identify vital elements in the operating systems and move toward description and measurement of them. In time, we can combine the study of program process with the study of outcomes. In the interim, it is not unimportant to know how the intended beneficiaries of the program are faring.

Evaluators used to yell and pound on the table that program staff should not wait to call them in until the program was in operation. They wanted not only to be in on the ground floor when the program was being planned; they wanted to "help dig the foundation." [9] Many program people have learned the lesson; evaluators are often in from the start. Now, however, it becomes clear that there is such a thing as premature evaluation. [10] Evaluations begin before the program has found its goals, its functions, or generally accepted ways of work. An analysis of the system can help program developers as they seek direction. It is a rewarding research activity, but it is not evaluation. Evaluation comes later, when there is an entity, however complex and interrelated, that can be defined, tested, and replicated. In the interests of social policy, we cannot postpone this part of the study too long.

If there is some recognizable set of principles and procedures that can be called a program, I am not sure that it is necessary to hold it steady in the arbitrary and argumentative way in which most raisers-of-the-issue propose. Programs almost inevitably drift. If the program and the drift are classified and analyzed, it seems possible to attribute the ensuing effects to the program in terms of how it worked and will often work in this disorderly world. Here are some suggestions that may be workable:

[9] Elizabeth Herzog, *Some Guide Lines for Evaluative Research* (Washington, D.C.: U.S. Department of Health, Education and Welfare, 1959), p. 84.
[10] Nelson Aldrich, ed., "The Controversy over the More Effective Schools: A Special Supplement," *Urban Review,* II, No. 6 (1968), 15–34. The evaluator himself believed that the study was premature.

1. Take frequent periodic measures of program effect (for example, monthly assessments in programs of education, training, therapy), rather than limiting collection of outcome data to one point in time.[11]
2. Encourage a clear transition from one program approach to another. If changes are going to be made, try to see that *A* is done for a set period, then *B,* then *C.*
3. Clarify the assumptions and procedures of each phase and classify them systematically.
4. Keep careful records of the persons who participated in each phase. Rather than lumping all participants together, analyze outcomes in terms of the phase(s) of program in which each person participated.
5. Press for a recycling of earlier program phases. Sometimes this happens naturally; on occasion, it can be engineered. If it is possible, it provides a way to check on earlier conclusions.
6. Seek to set aside funds and get approval for smaller-scale evaluation of (at least) one program phase or component that will remain stable for a given period.[12] For this venture, experimental procedures can be applied, even though less rigorous and more flexible methods may be sufficient in other program areas.
7. If nothing works and the program continues to meander (chaos would be the proper word in some contexts), consider jettisoning the evaluation framework in favor of meticulous analysis of the what, how, and why of events.

Relationships with Program Personnel

The evaluator works on the turf of another profession. His relationships with the program professionals (teachers, recreation workers, trainers, correction officers) can range from friendly and cooperative to extremes of hostility. Occasionally, an evaluation closes down before completion because of the effective resistance of operating program personnel. The more usual situation, however, is wary coexistence.

Sources of friction

What causes friction? There are many contributing factors.

Personality differences. Some observers cite the personality differences

---

[11] For example, Nathan Caplan, "Treatment Intervention and Reciprocal Interaction Effects," *Journal of Social Issues,* XXIV, No. 1 (1968), 63–88.

[12] For further discussion see Edward L. McDill, Mary S. McDill, and J. Timothy Sprehe, *Strategies for Success in Compensatory Education: An Appraisal of Evaluation Research* (Baltimore, Md.: The Johns Hopkins Press, 1969), pp. 66–71.

between people who go into program practice and those who go into research. The researcher is likely to be a detached individual, interested in ideas and abstractions. He thinks in terms of generalizations and analytical categories. His interest is in the long-term acquisition of knowledge, rather than the day-to-day issues of program operation. He seems cool, uncommitted to any program philosophy or position, without personal loyalties to the program or the organization. As Leonard Duhl has said, the researcher is a "marginal man."

The practitioner, on the other hand, is likely to be a warm, outgoing personality. (This at least is the common expectation in such service professions as teaching, therapy, health care, social work, and occupational counseling, although it is clearly not true of everyone and may not even be the norm in some occupations.) The practitioner generally is intensely concerned about people, specifics, the here and now. He is committed to action. He finds the researcher's skepticism uncongenial, and he finds it difficult to warm up to him as a human being.

Differences in role. Other observers believe that differences in role are more significant than any underlying personality variables. Basically, a practitioner has to believe in what he is doing; a researcher has to question it. This difference in perspective creates inevitable tensions.[13] Whatever their initial personal or value characteristics, once they go about their divergent tasks, they are almost bound to see things differently. Paula Kleinman tells a story about her experience as a graduate student working on a "training-and-evaluation" project. The project had a staff of four. At first they were assigned interchangeably to training and to evaluation tasks. Everyone got along very well, but there was concern that their commitment to the training program might "contaminate" the evaluation data. In the interest of objectivity, the group was divided in half, two people assuming training roles and the other two assigned to evaluation. Almost immediately, the comradely relationships deteriorated and dissension developed. The main issue was that the training group wanted to use the data from the preprogram questionnaires in later training sessions in order to enrich the

---

[13] See Hyman Rodman and Ralph L. Kolodny, "Organizational Strains in the Researcher-Practitioner Relationship," in *Applied Sociology: Opportunities and Problems,* ed. Alvin Gouldner and S. M. Miller (New York: The Free Press, 1965), pp. 93–113. For further discussion, see W. L. Slocum, "Sociological Research for Action Agencies: Some Guides and Hazards," *Rural Sociology,* XXI, No. 2 (1956), 196–99; Joel Smith, Francis M. Sim, and Robert C. Bealer, "Client Structure and the Research Process," in *Human Organization Research,* ed. R. N. Adams and J. J. Preiss (Homewood, Ill.: Dorsey Press, 1960), Chap. 4; William F. Whyte and Edith Hamilton, *Action Research for Management* (Homewood, Ill.: Dorsey Press, 1964), pp. 209–21.

training; the evaluators opposed the release of the data on grounds that trainees' knowledge of Time 1 answers might artificially alter Time 2 responses. Differences in role and responsibility had introduced frictions.

Lack of clear role definition. Evaluation often requires practitioners to take on new roles, such as referring people to the "experimental" program, adhering to the specific program approaches (curriculums, treatment modalities) being tested, collecting data, collaborating with the evaluator. The new roles may not be clearly defined in advance and become apparent only after a series of disputes with the evaluators. Even when roles are not new, the division of roles between practitioner and evaluator may be murky. Tensions can arise over differences in interpretation about who has responsibility for which functions. Particularly frustrating are uncertainties about the authority structure; it is often unclear who has authority to resolve the differences that arise.[14]

Conflicting goals, values, interests, frames of reference. The practitioner is concerned with service. He sees evaluation as a diversion and possibly even a threat. It seems to take things away from the program—money, time, administrators' attention—and promises the dubious return of a "report card." The evaluator, after all, is judging the value of his work, and by extension, his professional competence and *him*. The ultimate result of the evaluation, if it is used in decision making, will affect the future of his particular project and perhaps his own job. It may be perfectly true that the purpose of the evaluation is to add to knowledge and to rationalize social policy making, but it is he and his project who will bear the consequences if the results show project failure.

Sometimes practitioners see the evaluation as part and parcel of an innovation in programming that violates cherished concepts of service and tradition. They visit their dislike on both the program and its evaluation component. If the program runs counter to traditional agency values (for example, if it stresses social factors in the rehabilitation of mental patients when the accepted emphasis has been on psychological factors), they may actively or passively undermine the program and—as a consequence—the evaluation.

The practitioner sometimes questions the worth of the evaluator's research tools. He sees the measuring instruments as crude, good enough only to pick up gross changes. He doubts their ability to detect the subtle effects —such as growth in a person's self-confidence—that are vital effects of the

[14] Carol H. Weiss, *Organizational Constraints on Evaluation Research* (New York: Bureau of Applied Social Research, 1971).

program. The program practitioner on the spot sees growth and achievement that the evaluator, with his "insensitive measuring devices," misses.

On the other hand, of course, the practitioner is an interested party, and he may be seeing changes that are not actually there. While the practitioner levels charges of "insensitive indicators," the evaluator countercharges with "self-serving observation." There may be some element of truth on both sides, but the implications for the evaluator are clear. First, if he is to win the support of practitioners, he has to develop instruments that measure the factors that practitioners believe are the key effects of the program. They may believe that they deal in attitudes and values, perceptions and beliefs; if these are important program effects, he should find effective ways to measure them. Second, he may seek to convince practitioners that programs are almost always behavioral in intent. They aim to change what people *do*. His measuring tools will be designed to detect the vital effect—the change in behavior.

There is another aspect to this general resistance. In human service professions, practitioners deal with individuals. They are very much aware of individual differences, and they gain esteem and professional recognition from their sensitivity to the facets that differentiate one human being from another and their ability to tailor service to individual needs. The evaluator, on the other hand, deals in statistics—means, percentages, correlation coefficients—gross measures that lump people together. (He may, of course, break out the data by sex, age, race, length of program experience, and other factors, but that does not vitiate the practitioners' pervasive sense of mass data.) In confronting the evaluation data, the practitioner seldom sees that the conclusions are relevant to the specific people with whom he is working. It may be true, for example, that long periods of incarceration are associated with poor postprison adjustment, but the correctional officer cannot really believe that this datum deserves much weight when he has all his knowledge and experience and Johnny Jones standing in front of him.[15]

Institutional characteristics. When an agency has a history of internal conflict, evaluation may be viewed with particular suspicion. Staff are apt to see the evaluators as management hatchet men—or as the agents of one faction out to do in another. Evaluators' secrecy—their refusal to share data prematurely, their insistence on the confidentiality of individual records —may look threatening in a troubled organization. In fact, the staff of any agency where grievances are strong and satisfaction low may resent the evaluation as another cross to bear.

[15] See Francis G. Caro, "Approaches to Evaluative Research: A Review," *Human Organization,* XXVIII, No. 2 (1969), 87–99.

Other aspects of the institutional setting have consequences as well. Evaluator-practitioner relationships are affected by such aspects of the agency as the administrative structure, the fiscal and bookkeeping arrangements for the evaluation, supervisory practices, openness of communication channels, and the state of relationships with cooperating agencies who refer participants, receive referrals, or offer complementary services.[16] Where ambiguity and fragmented authority flourish, the evaluation is apt to suffer the strains of misperception, conflicting goals, and inadequate support.

Issues that lead to friction

What are the issues that provoke conflict?

Data collection. The request that practitioners administer questionnaires, interviews, and tests to clients is a frequent source of trouble. Often, the evaluator wants the practitioner too to fill out forms or submit to interviews and observation. The practitioner is trying to get a job done. He finds the intrusion time-consuming and disruptive.[17] Since he sees no obvious payoff to the program from the information collected (much of it looks like pretty abstruse and irrelevant stuff), he boggles at the amount of time away from the task at hand. Even when the evaluator has his own staff to collect the information, there are occasional conflicts over access to people, annoyance, and scheduling.

Changes in record-keeping procedures. If the evaluator seeks to collect information from the agency records, another set of squabbles may arise. The records are almost never complete enough and well enough kept for his purposes. (This appears to be a good generalization no matter what the type of agency.) Once he starts asking that practitioners get the records up to date and fill in the missing information, he encounters resistance. If in addition, he has the temerity to ask that the records be kept in a different form, with information items coded to suit the purposes of the evaluation, the disruption of established ways of work can create further friction.

Selection of program participants. The evaluator usually wants a say in how participants are selected for the program. He is likely to opt for some kind of random procedure. Practitioners, on the other hand, usually

[16] Conflicts over these issues and others are discussed in Gwen Andrew, "Some Observations on Management Problems in Applied Social Research," *The American Sociologist,* II, No. 2 (1967), 84–89, 92.

[17] A frustrating attempt to add the job of research interviewer to that of social caseworker is discussed in Michael A. LaSorte, "The Caseworker as Research Interviewer," *The American Sociologist,* III, No. 3 (1968), 222–25.

want to choose participants on the basis of their amenability to help, the seriousness of their need, or other obvious or subtle characteristics. Random procedures negate their professional skills of diagnosis and service planning. But what the practitioner sees as responsible individual selection makes the participant group "special" in unspecified ways, and thus makes comparison between participants and controls useless as an indication of program effect. Further, the evaluator does not know to what other populations the results are generalizable. Selection, then, is a common bone of contention.

Control groups. Another problem is control groups. Evaluators want them for the obvious purpose of ruling out rival explanations for the effects observed. Practitioners frequently regard them as a denial of service to needy people that violates all the ethical imperatives of service professions. Only when there are more applicants than available program slots are they likely to accept the researcher's requirements for controls. And when participants drop out of the program, it is not unknown for practitioners to raid the control group for new clients. Or they can upgrade services to controls who are supposedly receiving routine treatment in a competitive effort to "look good." It is difficult enough for evaluators to maintain contact and cooperation with controls who are not receiving the new showcase program, but when practitioners regard this as a "silly frill," they can further sabotage the effort.

Feedback of information into the program. Feedback—the communication of early evaluation information to affect later stages of the program—is another issue. Practitioners want to see the program improved by whatever means. If evaluation data can show them ways to increase effectiveness, they do not see why evaluators should object. (Isn't the purpose of evaluation to improve the program?) Of course, that may or may not be the purpose of a particular evaluation. When the purpose is longer range—for example, to decide on the worth of a particular program theory and approach—the evaluator wants the basic program model to remain stable for a long enough time to study its effects. He doesn't want his data to be used to shake things up drastically. But refusal to help is viewed as lack of commitment to the organization. The evaluator is refusing to come to grips with practical problems; he is not accepting any share of the responsibility for the program. (In the longer run, of course, when he has findings to report, he may play an active role. But in the interim, staff members see him as aloof and uncommitted.)

Status rivalry. Practitioners on occasion resent what they see as the higher status accorded researchers. They slave away and do the day-to-day drudgery, while the evaluator observes, measures, writes a report, and collects all the kudos—programmatic, academic, and sometimes financial as well.[18] As they see it, the evaluator asks them to make all the sacrifices while he collects all the rewards, through publication and professional recognition. They are likely to be particularly resentful when the evaluator produces the report, turns it in, and goes away without acknowledging any further obligation to the program. He appears to be milking the program of opportunities to further his own career without giving much in return.

Of course, should the evaluator try to get a hearing for his report in decision-making councils, some practitioners will not be happy, either. For them, the report usually means some kind of impending change. No evaluation report finds *everything* in perfect shape.[19] They may or may not agree with the cogency of the findings, but the almost inevitable implication is that they should change their ideas and procedures and perhaps learn new skills as well. Change is hard, and the evaluator who suggests it wins no popularity contest. If the evaluation is less than convincing, then they see little reason to depart from ways of work that have long stood them well.

Lessening the friction

This is an imposing catalog of sources of conflict, and it may seem that evaluators and practitioners are inevitably at odds. This is not necessarily so. With good communication and careful planning, most evaluations can proceed in a calm and cooperative atmosphere. If practitioners and evaluators rarely become close chums, they can usually settle their disputes in amicable fashion under appropriate conditions. When it comes time to put the results of evaluation into practice, differences may crop up again. We will return to the subject of the use of evaluation results in the next chapter. Here we will talk about ways of assuaging potential frictions.

Very little empirical research has been done on arrangements and methods that lessen tension in applied research projects. We therefore have to depend for guidance on the "received wisdom," the generally accepted lessons of experience. Six main conditions appear to be most successful in enabling people to function together comfortably.

Support from administrators. As previously mentioned, it is essential to involve project administrators and managers in planning an evaluation.

---

[18] For further discussion, see Rodman and Kolodny, *op. cit.*

[19] In fact, the tendency to negative findings is a common feature of evaluations to which we will return in the next chapter.

Through dialog with them, the evaluator develops insight and focus, and the administrators gain commitment to the study and to its eventual use in decision making. The support of top administrators is also crucial to getting and maintaining the cooperation of the program staff. They provide incentive, recognition, and reward for staff members who help, rather than hinder, the evaluation enterprise.

Involvement of practitioners in the evaluation. Involving the practitioners in planning the evaluation has further payoffs. A first benefit of bringing them in is that they gain understanding of what evaluation is all about. They learn what it is for and how it proceeds. This knowledge dispels some of the sense of threat (Why are they investigating what I'm doing?) and some of the suspicion generated by the presence of alien characters asking questions. Second, they have information and ideas to contribute. They can teach the norms of the project, the realities of its operation, and its jargon. Their contributions often enrich the evaluator's understanding and the sophistication of his study and make the evaluation more relevant to the needs of the agency. They can also keep him from making *faux pas* or unacceptable requests. Early consultation often forestalls later explosions. Further, they are more likely to be cooperative about new procedures and extra work when they see the sense of the requests. Thy are particularly likely to cooperate if they have had a chance to *contribute* to the development of the new procedures. When group meetings have been held and each member has seen group consensus develop on acceptance of the evaluator's requests, support for the study solidifies.

Although involvement in the early phases of the evaluation is important, it is equally necessary to continue communication through the life of the project. Each person whose work is affected by the evaluation should be kept informed and be given a chance to express his ideas and concerns. Whatever part the program staff plays during the course of the evaluation, the end of the study signals another opportunity for involvement. The evaluator has a responsibility to present his findings to the staff. He may find it stimulating, too, to ask for their help in interpreting the results and drawing conclusions for future action. He is not bound to accept their interpretations, but more than one investigator has found that they have interesting insights. Once they overcome their defensiveness, they can be useful colleagues in understanding the causes of past successes and failures, the process by which the program got where it is, what should be done in the future, and how to make future directions palatable to interested parties.[20]

[20] See M. A. Steward, "The Role and Function of Educational Research—I," *Educational Research,* IX, No. 1 (1966), 3–6.

Minimizing disruptions. Another tension reliever is adherence to the rules of the road. If evaluators have the good manners to recognize program priorities and limit their demands to indispensable issues, practitioners are likely to follow suit. The trick is to know which issues cannot be compromised and which are susceptible to negotiation. Far too often, evaluators impose heavier demands than their needs warrant. They ask eighty questions instead of twenty; they administer twelve batteries of tests when four would suffice. The reason is usually that they are not clear about what they are looking for, and they take all possible precautions not to miss anything that may turn out to be important. Better focus of the study at the outset—including clearer definition of the theory and expected process of the program—would lessen the zeal to cast a wide and undiscriminating net. Evaluators can become less of a nuisance as they become better informed.

Hiring research assistants to collect evaluation data, rather than asking already-burdened program staff to take on extra duties, is a good investment. Not only do they have more time and knowledge of research requirements, but their allegiance is not divided. Their commitment is to the quality of the data, not to the client or the program. When there is a separate research staff, however, the demarcation of duties should be clear to everyone. The researchers should not be suspected of invading the practitioners' domain or duplicating their work.

Emphasis on theory. Almost every evaluation is out to discover more than whether this particular program works in this particular time and place with this staff and these participants. Even the most practical manager wants to know whether it will work next year with different participants and some changes in staff and emphasis. It is important to be able to generalize about the basic approach that underlies the program. Is an educational film *as a technique* useful in changing people's use of medical services? Are small-group discussions more effective in changing attitudes on discrimination than lectures?

There is some kind of theory implicit in almost every program. If the evaluator can draw it to the surface and make it the central focus of the evaluation effort, he is on the way to alleviating the very real uneasiness that practitioners feel about being judged and having their performances critically rated. It is nice to think that if it is the *theory* of the program that is being judged, the practitioners can become eager partners in the investigation. This strikes me as overoptimistic. Practitioners realize that the evaluation, however theoretical in concept, is concerned with real events and can have real (and possibly baleful) consequences for the future of the program.[21] But an emphasis on theory can widen the perspective.

[21] Aronson and Sherwood, *op. cit.*

The feedback of useful information. If the evaluator can provide information that managers and practitioners need, he gains their support, even for some of his more bothersome and esoteric enterprises. Sometimes he can happily provide the information with no unpleasant side effects. But sometimes feedback, by changing subsequent program inputs or by contaminating later responses, would jeopardize his study. In that event, the best solution may be a separate data collection effort, apart from the evaluation, to satisfy program needs. In-house evaluation departments can do this more easily, both psychologically and financially, than outside research organizations, and they are more amenable to churning out the required data (and maybe even a speech or two for program people to give). This kind of practical side benefit can serve as an illustration of the utility of research data and increase practitioners' regard for the usefulness of the evaluator and his skills.

Clear role definitions and authority structure. People should know what is expected of them and of others. There should be clear understanding of the scope and limits of their roles. If practitioners perceive some of their obligations to be incompatible (for example, teaching to the best of their ability *and* using only the one instructional method being evaluated), ways should be found to communicate, interpret, and—if necessary—change role prescriptions in *advance* of the onset of the program.

When differences arise between program and evaluation personnel that cannot be reconciled by negotiation, the lines of authority should be clear.[22] Everyone should understand the channels of appeal and the person or group of persons who will make decisions. If interagency relations are involved, the situation may be complex but it is even more vital to establish clear lines of jurisdictional authority.[23]

The Social Context of the Program

Every program takes place in a setting that has consequences for its effectiveness. The primary context is the organization that sponsors and conducts the program. Even if the programs themselves are highly similar, one would expect differences between the outcomes of a community organization program run by the Chamber of Commerce and one run by a radical stu-

[22] For a case where the structure was unclear, see Hans Nagpaul, "The Development of Social Research in an Ad Hoc Community Welfare Organization," *Journal of Human Relations,* XIV, No. 4 (1966), 620–33.

[23] A first-rate analysis of this and related issues is given in D. B. Kandel and R. H. Williams, *Psychiatric Rehabilitation: Some Problems of Research* (New York: Atherton Press, Inc., 1964).

dent group, or between a foreign technical assistance program supported by the U.S. Department of Defense and one supported by UNESCO. Programs in turn have effects on the organizations that run them. The effects may be favorable (raising the prestige of the agency), competitive and draining (drawing the most competent and committed staff from the regular run of programs into the "special" program), destructive (diverting the organization from the mission at which it is skilled and enmeshing it in programs and conflicts it is poorly equipped to handle).

The larger social frameworks of neighborhood and community also affect programs and their consequences. So, too, do national systems of values, laws, and sensitivities. Family planning programs will be welcomed in one country and boycotted in another. Local mores even determine what can be studied and what cannot. Thus, new nations or those engaged in modernization may be extremely sensitive to studies revealing the extent of poverty or maldistribution of wealth.[24] In the United States, drug use is defined as a criminal activity. Programs for addicts have therefore been under pressure to regard abstinence from drug use as the only possible goal. Meyer and Bigman report that until recently, it was almost impossible for a program to aim for anything less than abstinence, or for evaluators to study program results in terms of improved social functioning without regard to whether the patient was on or off drugs.[25] Hardy souls have now raised questions about alternative goals and criteria of program success.

Just as the program is embedded in a social context, so too is the person who participates. He does not come to the program empty, unattached, or unanchored. He has beliefs and values, he has friends and relatives, habits, patterns of behavior, and ideas. Often the pull of his existing social arrangements work against the efforts of the program to bring about change. This may mean that program efforts are inundated by the flood of other influences which are part of his everyday routine. One implication for evaluation may be the value of exploring the supportive and inhibiting features of the interpersonal context. It might investigate the attitudes and behaviors of key people in the participant's environment (family, coworkers, teachers) during the time the program is trying to instill new patterns of behavior. For example, for in-service training programs that teach new styles of work, the responses of supervisors back on the job may be crucial for the retention or fade-out of the lessons taught. Brim found that among mothers urged to adopt new feeding practices, husbands' reactions—although they

24 Ralph L. Beals, *Politics of Social Research* (Chicago: Aldine-Atherton, Inc., 1969), p. 27.

25 Alan S. Meyer and Stanley K. Bigman, "Contextual Considerations in Evaluating Narcotic Addiction Control Programs," *Proceedings of the Social Statistics Section* (Washington, D.C.: American Statistical Association, 1968), pp. 175–80.

did not influence the probability of trying the advised procedures—were influential in continuation of the trials and eventual adoption of the new practices.[26] Unless participants receive support from their social environment, or are at least freed from some of its binds, program efforts may founder. The evaluator who locates the operative sources of support or obstruction can help program planners direct their attention to reaching and affecting these groups and thereby strengthen program impact.

Agencies are similarly affected by the pull of existing arrangements. Their efforts to run novel programs may run afoul of obligations to established constituencies, public reactions, or countervailing pressures. On the other hand, their most potent effects may be the rearrangement of traditional patterns of thought and behavior in other agencies. Legal service programs for the poor, for example, may have greater impact on the practices of public agencies that deal with poor people than their direct benefits to the clients themselves. Evaluation can find this out.

Evaluation need not be limited to local effects or low horizons. Sometimes the most important influences on a program's success lie outside the program's immediate purview. Sometimes the most important consequences of a program are not the effects on participants directly but on other people, agencies, or community institutions. The lesson for the evaluator is: Be alert. The studies that are ultimately most practical and useful are often those that open our eyes to new elements on the scene.

[26] Orville G. Brim, Jr., "The Acceptance of New Behavior in Child Rearing," *Human Relations,* VII (1954), 473–91.

6

Utilization of Evaluation Results

The evaluator, having survived the recurrent crises of the study, finally collects and analyzes his data and produces a report. He turns it in to the administrators of the program and the sponsors of the study and waits for the facts to speak for themselves. But often nothing happens. Why? He has heeded all the injunctions in the earlier chapters: He has gained commitment from administrators, geared the study to agency purposes, involved practitioners, conducted a methodologically competent study, and completed it in time for decisions, and still the results are ignored. A number of constraints frequently limit the use of evaluation results. We will take a look at five: (1) the evaluator's perception of his role in the utilization process, (2) the organization's resistances to change, (3) inadequate dissemination of results, (4) the gap between evaluation findings and clear courses for future action, and (5) the tendency of much evaluation to show little or no positive effect. In each case, we will discuss approaches for improving utilization.

The Evaluator's Role

Evaluators generally come out of the academic research tradition. In school they were subjected to the socialization processes and the initiation rites of science. By far the majority still take what Kathleen Archibald has described as an "academic orientation" to their work.[1] They value their autonomy from the sponsor's interference in their research, and once they have completed their study, they do not seek involvement in the agency's decision-making conflicts. If the facts don't speak for themselves, they have little intention of getting embroiled in the organization's political processes in order to speak *for* them.

Applied social researchers, whether they are employed by the program agency, a university, or a research organization, tend to look to the academic community for recognition and reward. Many evaluators are therefore more interested in doing work that will be of interest to their professional colleagues than in answering administrators' practical questions.[2] Even when the evaluator has conducted a responsible study in terms of agency purposes, his reward will come through publication in a respectable professional journal. He has little relish for spending nonresearch hours interpreting the results to decision makers and pleading their cause. The case of the RAND expert who conducted a study for the Air Force and then spent months fighting for its conclusions through the echelons of the Department of Defense [3] is looked on as an anomaly—and an object lesson of what can happen if a researcher gets caught up in the "utilization" game.

The academic orientation sometimes leads evaluators to stop short of drawing conclusions when they report their results. As they see it, their job is to conduct the study and analyze the data; it is not to recommend action. Since, as we shall discuss below, the implications of the data are rarely obvious, the evaluator's abdication of this task all too often means that nobody does it. The program manager winds up complaining about the irrelevance of the evaluation for his programmatic concerns, and the

[1] Kathleen A. Archibald, "Alternative Orientations to Social Science Utilization," *Social Science Information,* IX, No. 2 (1970), 7–34.

[2] See James A. Davis, "Great Books and Small Groups: An Informal History of a National Survey," in *Sociologists at Work: Essays on the Craft of Social Research,* ed. P. E. Hammond (New York: Basic Books, Inc., Publishers, 1964), pp. 212–34, for a discussion of this orientation.

[3] For a description of this event, see Bruce L. R. Smith, *The RAND Corporation* (Cambridge, Mass.: Harvard University Press, 1966), pp. 195–240.

evaluator retires to his office lamenting the neglect of his work by decision makers.[4]

When academically oriented evaluators look for solutions to the problem of nonutilization of their results, they come up with two: more social scientists in policy-making positions who will presumably pay more heed to research, and the development of a "middleman" role to serve as a link between applied researchers and decision makers. The recruitment to policy positions is clearly beyond the control of these advocates (and there may be some doubt that social-science training outweighs the political imperatives of the policy role). But the middleman, a reform that has been described and advocated for decades in field after field, should be more amenable to influence.[5] Nevertheless, in the immediate local setting, he is rarely in evidence.

The agency that runs the program which is being evaluated almost never has a resident agent who takes responsibility for translating and interpreting evaluation results. If the evaluator and the agency administrators opt out, the gulf between study and action looms large. On rare occasions, a consultant or board member who has been involved in the evaluation and is respected by the agency can help develop recommendations from the results—but this usually happens more by accident than by design. There is usually no permanent organizational base or authority, no professional role or recognized qualifications for the middleman.[6] Until appropriate structures and functions are developed (see the section on proposed remedies, following), the unwary soul who tries to bridge the gap may fall through it himself, or wind up as advocate for one side or the other.

An interesting feature of most writing on the middleman plan for overcoming the neglect of results is that it involves bringing in *other* people. It leaves the evaluator's uncommitted role intact. There are, however, minor-

4 Stake is not sure that the evaluation should make judgments. If he takes on this task, the evaluator (and social science research generally) will become even more suspect among practitioners than is now the case. He suggests that evaluators present the data and then seek and process the judgments of experts. Robert E. Stake, "The Countenance of Educational Evaluation," *Teachers College Record,* LXVIII, No. 7 (1967), 523–40.

5 For an excellent summary and analysis of this literature, see Ronald G. Havelock, "Dissemination and Translation Roles," in *Knowledge Production and Utilization in Educational Administration,* ed. Terry L. Eidell and Joanne M. Kitchel (Eugene, Ore.: Center for the Advanced Study of Educational Administration, 1968), pp. 64–119.

6 Havelock, *op. cit.* See also Ronald G. Havelock, *Planning for Innovation Through Dissemination and Utilization of Knowledge* (Ann Arbor, Mich.: Institute for Social Research, The University of Michigan Press, 1969).

ity traditions in applied research that place greater value on influencing the decision process. One of the best known is "action research." Derived principally from the work of Kurt Lewin, action research involves self-study procedures; the people who are to take action participate in the research process. The action-research group diagnoses its difficulties, collects information to help make necessary changes, and after the changes have been effected, evaluates their effectiveness. The research aspect is clearly subordinated to bringing about needed modifications in the structure and functioning of the group.

Even outside the action-research school, there is an increasingly vocal minority of evaluators who perceive their role as encompassing the "selling" of their results. They are willing to take time away from their research and publication activities in order to have an effect on the real world. They are interested in contributing to the rationalization of social policy and the improvement of social programming. If the researcher undertakes an evaluation, they believe he has a responsibility to make it relevant to the particular imperatives and constraints of the organization and to develop it in directions that contribute to the quality of the ensuing decisions. Longood and Simmel, for example, urge the evaluator to become an advocate for his results and to take part in the rough-and-tumble of organizational decision making.[7]

One reason, then, for the nonutilization of evaluation results may be the investigator's disinterest in following through. But why don't the organizations who have paid out sizable sums of money for the study take the initiative in putting it to use?

Organizational Resistances

Let us assume that the study results show that the program has led to moderate success with some groups, but pretty grievous failure elsewhere. The implication is that the organization had better make some drastic revisions. Somehow time drags on, and not a great deal happens. The reasons can be grouped under the headings of feasibility, acceptability and ideology.

[7] Robert Longood and Arnold Simmel, "Organizational Resistance to Innovation Suggested by Research," in *Evaluating Action Programs: Readings in Social Action and Education,* ed. Carol H. Weiss (Boston: Allyn & Bacon, Inc., 1972), pp. 311–17. See also Chris Argyris, "Creating Effective Research Relationships in Organizations," *Human Organization,* XVII, No. 1 (1958), 34–40; Floyd Mann and Rensis Likert, "The Need for Research on the Communication of Research Results," *Human Organization,* XI, No. 4 (1952), 15–19; Stanley Sadofsky, "Utilization of Evaluation Results: Feedback into the Action Program," in *Learning in Action,* ed. June L. Shmelzer (Washington, D.C.: Government Printing Office, 1966), pp. 22–36.

Feasibility

Organizations tend to find the status quo a contentedly feasible state. Changing organizational practices takes money, a factor often in short supply. It requires management effort and time. Often it requires changing the accustomed practices and habits of staff, who are satisfied with things as they are and who believe in their present way of working. If new skills are needed, this will take retraining of old staff (again time, money, a break in comfortable routines) or the employment of new people (who must be found, attracted, paid, and kept). In short, an organization is a complex social system. It has built up a pattern of staff role behaviors and a system of motivation and rewards for compliance with existing roles. It is not sure that it will be successful in instituting new patterns. Small wonder that the organization wants to be convinced that new practices will have significantly better outcomes than old ways before it disrupts existing arrangements.

Further, organizations have concerns other than achieving their goals. They are interested in survival. They want to generate support, maintain their position in the political and interorganizational environment, satisfy their constituencies. Nor should these survival concerns necessarily be viewed as antithetical to the achievement of goals. Although they can contribute to organizational rigidity, they are also in one sense preconditions for effective activity. The organization is building up strength and credits for the future. Managements sometimes fear that too much change, too frequent or too drastic, will lead to instability, a lack of direction, and a loss of confidence in the organization's capabilities. These are authentic concerns.

Acceptability

Another set of issues has to do with the acceptability of new practices to outside groups. Revisions in program may cause changes in relationships to funders, clients, other community organizations. There is a chance that the changes will not be acceptable. If they conflict with current expectations and fail to satisfy the interests of these groups, the organization may be in for a period of struggle and chaotic adjustment.

Further, new practices may not fit in with prevailing social values. For example, a recommendation to concentrate resources in slum schools may meet resistance from middle-class taxpayers. Even if proposed changes would help to improve achievement of program goals, it is perfectly possible that they will have deleterious side effects and create new kinds of problems. Lack of certainty about the acceptance of the recommendations outside the agency can be an effective inhibitor of change. The importance of getting and maintaining Congressional support for federal social programs is a recurrent issue.

Ideology

Organizations have ideological commitments. They tend to believe in a set of values and even in particular methods of work. Any conclusions that threaten their basic allegiances are likely to receive short shrift. Thus, studies that discount the effectiveness of open enrollment or graduate fellowships or that suggest alternatives to individual psychotherapy meet with resistance from agencies committed to these values and procedures. When one evaluation showed that a group work program for potentially delinquent high school girls was ineffective in preventing delinquent behavior, the agency response was to suggest an increase in the number of group sessions per week. Wherever strong ideological commitments are involved (particularly to basic beliefs in equality and justice), even totally negative results will not lead to abandonment of programs; evaluation must offer guidance for improving the way programs meet their goals.

Even when all these considerations are viewed with sympathy, some organizations put up excessive resistance to change. Unlike profit-making businesses whose fate is decided by the balance sheet, service agencies are not seriously penalized for failing to reach their goals. Budgetary allotments or private contributions keep flowing in. If the clientele are discontented, they have little effective voice in the running of things. Sometimes not knowing they are shortchanged, they are happy just to have someone paying attention to them. Certainly, conscientious administrators want to do good as well as do well, but they can find cheerful rationalizations for persisting in an unproductive course ("the poor showing is temporary"; "it's the result of outside conditions"; "all we need is more money"; "the evaluation isn't very good anyway"). Criticism of methodology is an increasingly common counterattack against unfavorable evaluation.[8]

[8] Two recent cases are the criticisms of the Westinghouse-Ohio University national evaluation of Head Start and the controversy over the More Effective Schools evaluation in New York City. Walter Williams and John W. Evans, "The Politics of Evaluation: The Case of Head Start," *Annals of the American Academy of Political and Social Science*, Vol. 385 (September 1969), 118–32; Nelson Aldrich, ed., "The Controversy over the More Effective Schools: A Special Supplement," *Urban Review*, II, No. 6 (1968), 15–34. In both cases, evaluators concede that some of the methodological criticism is justified; they operated under restrictions that prevented ideal design. Nevertheless, it appears likely that the criticism was motivated more by ideology than by methodology—that critics wanted to protect a popular program. Had the evaluation results been favorable, it is hard to imagine a similar outcry.

Proposed organizational remedies

Observers have proposed remedies for the resistance to evaluation results. Campbell, for example, says:

> One simple shift in political posture which would reduce the problem is the shift from the advocacy of a specific reform to the advocacy of persistence in alternative reform efforts should the first one fail. The political stance would become: "This is a serious problem. We propose to initiate Policy A on an experimental basis. If after five years there has been no significant improvement, we will shift to Policy B." [9]

Attractive as the proposal is, it does not appear "simple." All our experience suggests that groups engaged in reform have to *believe* in what they advocate if they are to weather the political struggles, and that decision makers have to be *convinced* that the plan is good and right and worth the investment. Rivlin notes:

> The Office of Economic Opportunity might have told Congress: "We don't know whether preschool programs will work, or what kind would be best, but we have designed a program to find out." But would they then have gotten the money? [10]

Further, administrators and program staff become committed to the programs to which they devote their energies. Such dedication is probably important for their success as practitioners; a skeptical wait-and-see posture might well hobble their effectiveness in action. They, and sometimes program participants as well, develop vested interests in the program. Other political interests, too, congregate around things as they are. But perhaps on a small-scale basis, when resources are scarce, or when the "pro" and "anti" forces are finely balanced (and out of expediency as much as rationality), contemporary policy makers will come to allow program trials with appropriate evaluation of effects before they ·embark on major reforms. Recent experiments with guaranteed income plans are a hopeful sign that such an approach is possible. [11]

[9] Donald T. Campbell, "Reforms as Experiments," *American Psychologist*, XXIV, No. 4 (1969), 410.

[10] Alice M. Rivlin, *Systematic Thinking for Social Action* (Washington, D.C.: The Brookings Institution, 1971), p. 85.

[11] See "Preliminary Results of the New Jersey Graduated Work Incentive Experiment" (Washington, D.C.: Office of Economic Opportunity, February 1970), and "Further Preliminary Results of the New Jersey Graduated Work Incentive Experiment" (Washington, D.C.: Office of Economic Opportunity, May 1971).

Moreover, this is a fast-moving world. Community conditions and aspirations change. New people come into leadership positions in agencies. Outside review stimulates organizational self-analysis. What was once immutable becomes the subject for debate.[12] Evaluation evidence may be taken down from the shelf and gather partisans; new studies may be commissioned. When organization personnel are dissatisfied with things as they are, they are more receptive to the implications of evaluation results. It is a state of puzzlement and dissatisfaction that sometimes leads to evaluation in the first place, and under these conditions, the results are apt to be taken seriously.[13] Perhaps our expectations for the use of results have had too short a time frame. It probably takes a period before conclusions come into currency and gain support, and organizations mobilize resources for action.

Agency channels. The fact remains that more effective techniques are needed to persuade organizations to give evaluation results a hearing. The best way we know of to date is through the efforts of the determined administrator who insists that results be used to reach peak performance and who rewards the staff members who adapt.[14] Elsewhere I have proposed systematic study of a number of other techniques that might increase utilization, such as early identification of potential users and selection of issues of concern to them, involvement of staff members in planning and conducting the study, and participation by key outsiders who can spread the word or exert pressure on the organization.[15] Archibald suggests that the "planned change" or "human relations" approach to organizations associated with Lippitt, Bennis et al. might be enlisted in support of analysis and evalua-

[12] George James, "Planning and Evaluation of Health Programs," in *Administration of Community Health Services* (Chicago: International City Managers Association, 1961), pp. 114–34.

[13] Likert and Lippitt discuss problem sensitivity, an "image of potentiality" which implies that conditions can be changed for the better, and an experimental attitude toward innovation as preconditions for use of social science results. Rensis Likert and Ronald Lippitt, "The Utilization of Social Science," in *Research Methods in the Behavioral Sciences,* ed. Leon Festinger and Daniel Katz (New York: Holt, Rinehart & Winston Inc., 1953).

[14] See Ronald Lippitt, Jeanne Watson, and Bruce Westley, *The Dynamics of Planned Change* (New York: Harcourt Brace Jovanovich, Inc., 1958); Warren G. Bennis, Kenneth D. Benne, and Robert Chin, eds., *The Planning of Change,* 2nd ed. (New York: Holt, Rinehart & Winston, Inc., 1969), for discussion of other methods for fostering organizational change.

[15] Carol H. Weiss, "The Utilization of Evaluation: Toward Comparative Study," in *The Use of Social Research in Federal Domestic Programs,* Vol. III, U.S. Congress, House Committee on Government Operations, Research and Technical Programs Subcommittee, 90th Congress, 1st Session (Washington, D.C.: Government Printing Office, 1967), pp. 426–32.

tion.[16] The "planned change" school has traditionally concentrated on opening channels of communication, helping the organization recognize and work through its problems, and generating internal acceptance for change. "Change agents" have usually been outside consultants called in at a time of organizational crisis to act as diagnosticians and enablers, and they have been little concerned with the content of alternative actions or their real-world consequences. Despite the conceptual and operational differences between the approaches of "planned change" and "use of evaluation results," there seems to be merit in the notion of supplementing the rational appeal of evidence with attention to the group dynamics of the change process. The trick will be in meshing the two approaches—and finding staff with dual skills.

Incentives and rewards. Another avenue for increasing organizational attention to evaluation is to build appropriate incentives and rewards into program arrangements. One example is performance contracting. In this still-experimental system, an agency is paid only if it achieves certain set goals. Thus, an educational contractor is reimbursed for teaching children only to the extent that the children's achievement improves. Whatever its other risks, such a system demands use of evaluative data. Similar schemes have been proposed for developing evaluative criteria for hospital care, on-the-job training, and the like, and making adherence to these criteria a basis for determining the amount of federal support.[17] If federal social programs are decentralized to cities and if local groups obtain a greater voice in their control, such proposals may become increasingly attractive to federal policy makers as a way of seeing that goals are met. That such schemes may have other perverse consequences seems clear, and much analysis and experimentation should precede their adoption. But they represent one possible way to enlarge what are now generally feeble rewards for giving evaluation results a place in the action.

Proposed voucher systems are another, somewhat less direct, way of rewarding attention to evaluative outcomes. Clients are given vouchers for services, and instead of becoming willy-nilly recipients of monopolistic public services (education, public housing, welfare counseling), they can choose their own services and pay for them with the vouchers. By introducing a competitive market, this plan would give clients a degree of control. Possibly they would be more interested in data on the relative effec-

---

16 K. A. Archibald, "Three Views of the Expert's Role in Policy-making: Systems Analysis, Incrementalism, and the Clinical Approach," *Policy Sciences,* I (1970), 73–86.

17 Charles L. Schultze, *The Politics and Economics of Government Spending* (Washington, D.C.: The Brookings Institution, 1968), pp. 103–25.

tiveness of different services than the service institutions themselves have been. They will need some sophistication, but they have the motivation to pay attention.

Presenting appropriate results to appropriate users. One of the major issues in promoting use of evaluation findings is getting information to the level of decision-maker who makes relevant program decisions. As we noted in Chapter 2, program managers do not usually decide whether a program continues or ends, or is reduced in scope or extended to other units. Rather they are involved in issues of operation such as the choice of strategies, staff, intensiveness of service, and the like. An evaluation report which says only that the program has not produced the expected effects is not of much use to them; this is the wrong order of information for their purposes. It may be appropriate information for top policy-makers, but program managers need data on relative effectiveness of different strategies if they are to use results constructively.

Presenting useful comparisons. Moreover, the evaluation should provide comparisons that are relevant to decisional alternatives. If *none* of the pending alternatives is to offer no service at all, a study which compared participants with controls who received no service will have limited applicability. More useful information would emerge from comparisons between program participants and: (1) recipients of the routine type of service, (2) recipients of scaled-down, inexpensive versions of the program under study, or (3) recipients of alternative types of innovative services. This would provide a basis for choosing among alternative courses of action. Clearly, some of the problems in organizational use of results derive from the evaluation itself.

Timing of the report. Evaluation conclusions are sometimes reported after decisions are made. This lack of fit with the decisional timetable may be due to a variety of factors in the situational context, in the organization, and in the evaluation. An issue may suddenly explode; lack of foresight about the need for evaluation may have led to a late start; delays occur in the conduct of the study; analysis of data often takes longer than the time allotted. Whatever the reason, organizations cannot use results responsibly when they appear late or when only the skeletal outlines of the data are ready in time for decision-making and the richness of detailed analysis is postponed—or forgone. Careful advance planning for evaluation, based on knowledge of what research entails and how long it takes, would help to circumvent the timing problem. Evaluators, too, have a responsibility to produce relevant results on time and save the explorations of intriguing byways for a later date.

Candor about limitations in the research. We have discussed the organizational resistances to evaluative results. Evaluators are not immune
to resistances of their own. Studies frequently have some deficiencies—in
conceptualization, measurement, design, or analysis—that limit their applicability. Yet evaluators have been known to defend even questionable
aspects of their work with the ardor of someone denying allegations of
immorality. A little more candor is called for. If there are gaps, rival interpretations, or room for doubt, the evaluator who acknowledges limitations
can help decision-makers arrive at responsible choices. Perhaps further
analysis of available data or collection of additional data can resolve the
question at issue. In the interim, decisions will not be set in concrete.

Communication of results. The evaluation report is often written in
the technical language of the researcher. To the organizational reader, not
only its terms but its conceptual perspective may be unfamiliar and con-
fusing. A report that hopes to shape decisions should be written in a style
that communicates to its audience. A short summary is usually advisable,
highlighting major findings and their implications (without scanting important qualifiers and unresolved issues), perhaps with some attention to
attractiveness of format and graphic display. Such "packaging" that smacks
of Madison Avenue appears demeaning to many researchers, a deviation
from their professional role. In such cases, a professional writer with social
science training may be hired to prepare the summary; the full report is
available to anyone who wants to probe deeper.

Planning and development units. We have noted the usual absence of
an agency middleman who bridges the gap between evaluation and administration and the fact that his absence is due in large measure to the lack
of an institutional base, authority, and a recognized role. If these were
provided in the internal structure of the organization, the middleman might
be legitimated—and recruited.[18]

The most feasible structure for allying evaluation with program seems
to be a program planning and development unit. This unit has the job of

[18] Even without a permanent institutional base, occasional individuals, committees, projects, and centers have brought research findings to the attention of users.
Ralph Nader is an individual who has performed an essentially evaluative role in
consumer education. Temporary committees, such as the Physical Science Study
Committee, have been highly effective in promoting adoption of curriculums and
other forms of knowledge. B. R. Clark, "Interorganizational Patterns in Education,"
Administrative Science Quarterly, X, No. 2 (1965), 224–37. National commissions
can contract for research and report results to a wide audience, e.g., the Riot Commission studies. National Advisory Commission on Civil Disorders, *Supplemental
Studies* (Washington, D.C.: Government Printing Office, 1968). University faculty
members can spread research results through their teaching and consultant activities.

continuous program development and improvement. If the agency takes such functions seriously, the unit would be high in the hierarchy, perhaps attached to the director's office. It would review the agency mission, consider indicators of effectiveness, propose modifications of program or new plans, and perhaps carry some responsibility for budget development as well. The evaluator would become an important source of information and support. When his reports feed into an ongoing planning function, he has leverage on the system.

Up until now, units of this type have been installed mainly in cases where an agency must submit annual plans for annual funding. They are fairly common in federal agencies, which must submit plans and budgets each year to the Congress, and in organizations where some version of the planning-programming-budgeting system provides a clear framework and set of procedures. Their introduction into operating programs at other levels might help to get evaluation into the organizational mainstream. But they must have the administrator's support—and his ear—and prove their worth in action, or we are merely moving the utilization problem from one location to another.

Better Dissemination of Evaluation Results

Much of our discussion has assumed that there are two stock characters (with a few supporting players) in our cast—an evaluator who produces research results of some degree of cogency and an agency policy maker who proceeds to ignore them. Fortunately, there are other actors in the drama. In some cases, the pivotal ones are policy-makers at superordinate levels (officials of federal agencies, the Congress). As we noted in Chapter 2, it is top policy makers who generally make decisions about allocation of resources and the continuation or termination of programs. If it is fruitless to present evaluation results to an operating agency—particularly negative results whose implication is that it should shut up shop—policy makers will often give them a hearing. With fewer commitments to things as they are, they are likely to be less biased and more willing to consider evidence of program effectiveness. This will not be their only basis for decision; they too have concerns about political palatability, feasibility, ideology, and costs. But they have the authority, and sometimes the motivation, to make appropriate decisions.

Other potential users are policy-makers in similar agencies (other boards of education, directors of other state conservation departments, directors of other hospitals). Even when decision makers in the agency whose program is evaluated balk at using the results or use them only to tinker with operations, these other actors have an interest in the proceedings. They, too, propose, fund, run, and supervise programs, and they have a stake in more effective social services. When a crisis blows up in their domain, or sticky problems arise, they will need information on other programs and the extent to which they have succeeded or failed under given conditions. They can learn from their counterpart's evaluation efforts. With fewer vested interests and sensitivities than the agency studied directly, they may have less resistance to the findings. On the other hand, since their situation is not likely to be identical, the application of the findings may involve adaptation rather than outright adoption.

Much of the use that is made of social research is by organizations other than the local "client" of the study. Evaluation done in connection with special demonstration programs, for example, may have little effect on local events because the life of the demonstration ends when the federal (or foundation) funding is up. The evaluation stops then, too, and rarely has a chance to affect decisions about local continuation of the program. But results of demonstration-project evaluation are useful to others. Federal and state agencies, and foundations and national organizations that set standards, disseminate information, propose new solutions to local problems, and fund local efforts need to know what works and what does not work under varying conditions so that they can support and propagate the most effective models. Legislators considering new social legislation and the extension of old programs can use the demonstration evaluations as one clue to wise allocation of resources. Clients of the program, and community groups generally, are another audience. They may have particular interest in evaluation results that show ways to improve the services they receive. If they can be reached with research evidence and their support mobilized, they may be able to exert pressure on agencies to put findings to effective use.

In order for any of these uses to occur, evaluation results must be communicated. This is a platitude, but it is far from common practice. Most evaluation reports seem to wind up as forty mimeographed copies, 400 pages long, submitted to a program or a funding agency and piled on a shelf. With notable exceptions, relatively few evaluation reports are transmuted into articles in professional journals or books. Sometimes the agency is responsible, demanding confidentiality as a condition of cooperation. Sometimes the study has been so compromised during its conduct that it is not a reputable piece of scholarship. On occasion, the evaluator is too weary and frustrated by the tribulations of the research process to salvage the important findings. He may see little generalizability of the results beyond the immediate case. Sometimes it is publishers and journals who are unreceptive to papers on evaluation topics. They see evaluation as dealing in particularized, atheoretical, practical information that adds little to the store of the world's knowledge. As evaluation stresses its conceptual as well as its workaday bases and analyzes significant social components, this professional inhospitability may change and evaluators may be motivated to do more professional writing.

For the time being, other outlets must be sought as well. Information briefs, abstracts of evaluation reports, selective annotated bibliographies—information systems of this type can be and in some places are being set up to apprise appropriate audiences about available reports. They should be selective, so as not to inundate readers with a mass of information of varying quality, much of which is not worth their attention. They have to reach the people who make the decisions. Then the reports have to be better—more readable, shorter, more attractive—and more readily available if information is to flow. Personal contact is an even better way to reach people. One study found that utilization of information on successful demonstrations was enhanced by attendance at conferences where potential users could discuss the program with program operators and by site visits where they could see it in operation.[19] Consultants from federal or state agencies (or from universities or private firms) can also make information visible and spur the utilization process.

Recently several federal agencies have established staffs of research utilization field agents. The model has been the Agricultural Extension Service with its system of county agents. In large decentralized operations, this seems to be the only feasible way to get evaluation results out to the field. The Social and Rehabilitation Service of the Department of Health, Education and Welfare and the Office of Education have both attached utilization agents to state agencies.[20] Their job is not viewed as repackaging significant research results in palatable forms and distributing them to po-

[19] Edward M. Glaser and Hubert S. Coffey, *Utilization of Applicable Research and Demonstration Results* (Los Angeles: Human Interaction Research Institute, 1967). A later report, however, shows that while conferences and consultation can generate enthusiasm, they are not enough to bring about adoption of new practices when money, personnel, and facilities are needed. See Edward M. Glaser and Harvey L. Ross, *Increasing the Utilization of Applied Research Results* (Los Angeles: Human Interaction Research Institute, 1971).

[20] For the Social and Rehabilitation Service, see George A. Engstrom, "Research Utilization: The Challenge of Applying SRS Research," *Welfare in Review*, VIII, No. 5 (1970), 1–7; Margaret F. Clark, "Creating a New Role: The Research Utilization Specialist," *Rehabilitation Record*, X, No. 6 (1969), 32–36. For the Office of Education Pilot State Dissemination Program, a brief notice appears in *Report on Education Research*, July 22, 1970, p. 6. See also Sam D. Sieber, "Activities of Field Agents in the U.S.O.E. Pilot State Dissemination Program" (New York: Bureau of Applied Social Research, March 1971).

tential users. Rather the utilization agent role is one of consultation and problem-solving. Agents help local agencies define their problems and their knowledge needs, retrieve relevant research through resource systems, and aid the agency to adapt the information to their purposes. As these systems develop, agents may become involved in helping agencies to implement programs based on research results. Their emphasis is not only on disseminating reports of successful programs but on sharing negative and equivocal results as well, and making available data that fit the conditions of the local operation.

The utilization programs are new and much remains to be done in developing roles, defining relations among agencies, and setting reasonable expectations. Nevertheless, they mark a hopeful advance in the development of the middleman between researcher and user.

We are learning in our studies of research utilization that it is fruitless to try to cram research results down the throats of people who are uninterested. On the other hand, when people face a decision, they often search for relevant information.[21] Even if they are seeking information to bolster a preconceived viewpoint, the dissemination system serves a useful function. By arming decision makers whose views coincide with research results with persuasive ammunition to fight their case, the system gets research a hearing—and a partisan.

The search for effective dissemination strategies is by no means over. Much remains to be done in each substantive field to make evaluation information available when it is needed.

The Gap Between Evaluation and
Action Recommendations

We have been assuming in this discussion that evaluation results have indicated a clear path for improvement. Sometimes this is not the case. Even with the use of experimental designs, process models, and sophisticated analytical techniques, there are times when an evaluation report can say little more than "The program is not achieving the desired results." How does one draw conclusions or take action on that basis?

Of course, the horizon is rarely so bleak. We usually do know such things as that one type of program service has been somewhat more effective than another, that girls have done better than boys, community-spon-

21 E.g., Carol H. Weiss, *The Consequences of the Study of Federal Student Loan Programs: A Case Study in the Utilization of Social Research* (New York: Bureau of Applied Social Research, 1970).

sored activities better than state-sponsored, experienced workers better than new ones. There is some pattern of data that will give rise to clues for improvement. But if the differences are small, they may offer a tenuous foundation on which to erect an elaborate superstructure of recommendations. Since he is involved with real people and serious organizational consequences, it would be a foolhardy evaluator who would spin grand utopian schemes out of a set of minor percentage differences. (He may be tempted to spin them out of his own ideology; that is a matter we will consider below.) An evaluation, then, points out weaknesses, but often offers only the barest hints for solution. There is a gap between data and action that will have to be filled in with intuition, experience, gleanings from the research literature, assumptions based on theory, ideology, and a certain amount of plain guessing. Moving through this gap to new program experimentation requires a commitment by decision makers to the belief that a new trial is better than continuation of a proven error.

Evaluation will never provide all the answers. What it can do—and this is no minor contribution—is expose the failings of existing programs and point out the need for change. It can sometimes get publicity for the failures (and successes) of programs, help to generate interest in program effectiveness outside the narrow confines of the agency, and provide support for those reformers who seek to improve program operations. Maybe the most practical use of evaluation findings is to provide hard evidence to support the proponents of change within the decision-making system—the people within and outside the agency who have been seeking to alter present modes of programming. Study data legitimate their cause and give them chapter and verse to cite. Another major contribution is raising new issues and altering the nature and climate of discussion. Over time, a recurrent pattern of evaluation findings can gradually work changes in public and professional opinion.

Evaluation can also, with varying degrees of confidence, offer alternatives to current operation. Some alternative proposals can be buttressed with hard data and clear support—for example, the rehabilitation programs in Centers A and D are clearly functioning better than those in Centers B and C. Sometimes the evidence is wispier. On occasion, there is no evidence, and the evaluator draws on his professional knowledge for offering alternatives to present courses of action. There is no rule of thumb for how far afield he should go, how far he should depart from the data to speculate on alternatives. The circumstances of the program and the agency, and his own bent, will determine the kinds of latitude that are feasible. If he knows a great deal about the field, has had previous experience with similar organizational activities, and is *persona grata* to the sponsor of the study, he can expatiate freely, with much benefit likely for the program. He will usually offer a range of suggestions, rather than just one, for accomplishing the purposes found unaccomplished.

But when the evaluator is drawing on knowledge and values outside the evaluation study, he has a responsibility to say so. It behooves him to indicate explicitly the extent to which the recommendations he offers are supported by study data, how far they are logical extensions of the data, and where he has taken off on his own. When he is making assumptions based on ideological positions, he can serve the cause of clarity by making his assumption and the basis for it explicit. Decision makers are thus helped to separate the evaluator's *obiter dicta* from the research results. If they disagree with the recommendations, they are not absolved from paying serious attention to the data.

There is even a step beyond suggesting alternative courses of action. The conscientious evaluator can proceed to an analysis of the likely consequences, good and bad, of the alternative courses he recommends. Particularly if the suggestions are dramatically divergent from current modes, an educated look at possible consequences is useful stuff to have. But by this point in our discussion, we have moved beyond his contributions as an evaluator into the realm of his contributions as a policy analyst and a participant in the decision-making process.

The Effect of "Little Effect"

One of the most serious impediments to putting evaluation results to use is their dismaying tendency to show that the program has had little effect. As Elinson notes,[22] competent evaluations have come out with negative results in field after field. This has been true in psychotherapy, corrections, casework, compensatory education, public housing—most of the fields that have received serious evaluation attention. The evaluator is thus in the position of turning thumbs down on someone's program. Since old, established programs are rarely evaluated, it is the venturesome program that bears the brunt. The negative cast of evaluation results has the effect of undermining reformers and innovative programs. Barnacle-encrusted programs—many of which would profit from a long, clear look—sit by unexamined. Observers note that the emotional effect of much evaluation is to give aid and

[22] Jack Elinson, "Effectiveness of Social Action Programs in Health and Welfare," in *Assessing the Effectiveness of Child Health Services, Report of the Fifty-sixth Ross Conference on Pediatric Research* (Columbus, O.: Ross Laboratories, 1967), pp. 77–81.

comfort to the barbarians, although the practical results are probably nil. Programs seem to survive regardless.

An unusually rigorous evaluation of a group counseling program for prison inmates found that outcomes for participants were no better than for controls.[23] The state department of corrections not only did not close the program, they extended it to every prison in the department and made inmate participation in some institutions compulsory. Ward and Kassebaum, the evaluators, suspect that the major response to the findings will be to restrict access to the prisons to outside researchers. The department will try to use its own staff for evaluation and then limit circulation of disappointing reports.[24]

The proclivity to the negative probably makes sophisticated program administrators and practitioners increasingly wary of the "contributions" of evaluation. As the word gets around, social programs may become generally less hospitable to evaluation. Another line of defense is to develop plausible counterclaims for programs that evaluation has found unsuccessful. Stember, facing the data that classroom integration has not had positive results on racial attitudes or on learning, asks why decisions should be affected by results on these criteria. Integration is ethically and legally right as a principle of democracy.[25] Similarly, Lerman finds that treatment programs in institutions for delinquents apparently have no appreciable effect on reducing the rate at which released delinquents get into further trouble with the law. Nevertheless, he concludes that treatment programs should be retained, because they do not *increase* failure rates and are more humane.[26] Both conclusions sound reasonable, but in similar ways the basic rationale for any ineffective program can be shifted without doing the hard intellectual and developmental work required to produce programs that work.

The pervasiveness of null results in evaluation research has serious implications for social policy in the broadest sense. It indicates that many of our social change efforts are poorly conceived and implemented. The easy parts of the job have been done in education, health, and other fields. As

[23] David A. Ward and Gene G. Kassebaum, "On Biting the Hand That Feeds: Some Implications of Sociological Evaluations of Correctional Effectiveness," in *Evaluating Action Programs: Readings in Social Action and Education,* ed. Carol H. Weiss (Boston: Allyn & Bacon, Inc., 1972), pp. 300–310.

[24] *Ibid.,* pp. 308–10.

[25] Charles H. Stember, "Evaluating Effects of the Integrated Classroom," *Urban Review,* II, No. 7 (1968), 3–4, 30–31.

[26] Paul Lerman, "Evaluative Studies of Institutions for Delinquents: Implications for Research and Social Policy," *Social Work,* XII, No. 4 (1968), 55–64.

we tackle the remaining problems, diminishing returns set in. It is increasingly hard to make headway. But as a society we are loath to abandon procedures that once appeared to work well.

Evaluation with its spate of negative results is delivering a vital message. Old ideas and old ways are not working in many critical fields. Social intervention is plagued with a series of important (but not necessarily insurmountable) shortcomings. One is the state of social science knowledge. Programs based on intuitive wisdom and extrapolations from past experience are not good enough. Important theoretical and research contributions are due. Even with the present state of knowledge, programs do not put into practice all that is known. Most programs are born with roots in existing agencies, traditional professions, established procedural arrangements. Rather than innovative programming, there is tinkering with the mixture as before. Moreover, programs are often poorly managed. There has been insufficient attention in many fields to developing the kinds of administrative skills that lead to optimal use of time and talent. The structure of programs, too, has often been deficient. Fragmentary projects are created to deal with broad-spectrum problems. Each program tackles one facet of a complex, interrelated issue, not only uncoordinated with complementary efforts but often competing and jockeying for power and prestige. Moynihan has recently contended that current conditions call for integrated policies rather than piecemeal programs. The day when a single program, however large in scale, could effectively solve serious social ills is coming to an end.[27]

Much remains to be done to improve social programming. Many moderate, piecemeal, cheap solutions have been tried, and evaluation research has found them wanting. If we take evaluation results seriously, we will have to embark on more fundamental social experimentation.[28] Social institutions will have to take greater risks in the search for effective programs. Evaluation can be a partner in this search if it is given the funds and the conditions to test out small-scale experimental projects. As programs are developed on better knowledge foundations, with better structural arrangements and greater integration with allied institutions and overall policies, evaluation has a further role to play. It can gauge the effectiveness of the innovations and determine which features are ineffective and which should be retained for further development. With all its failings, evaluation research still has the potential for bringing greater rationality to social decision making.

[27] Daniel P. Moynihan, "Policy vs. Program in the '70's," *The Public Interest,* No. 20 (1970), 90–100.

[28] Carol H. Weiss, "The Politicization of Evaluation Research," *Journal of Social Issues,* XXVI, No. 4 (1970), 57–68.

Bibliography

Conceptual and Methodological Issues

AGENCY FOR INTERNATIONAL DEVELOPMENT. *Evaluation Handbook*. Washington, D.C.: Government Printing Office, 1971.

ALKIN, MARVIN C. "Evaluation Theory Development," *Evaluation Comment*, II, No. 1 (1969), 2–7.

AMERICAN INSTITUTES FOR RESEARCH. *Evaluative Research Strategies and Methods*. Pittsburgh, Pa.: American Institutes for Research, 1970.

ANDREW, GWEN. "Some Observations on Management Problems in Applied Social Research," *The American Sociologist*, II, No. 2 (1967), 84–89, 92.

ARCHIBALD, K. A. "Three Views of the Expert's Role in Policy-making: Systems Analysis, Incrementalism, and the Clinical Approach," *Policy Sciences*, I (1970), 73–86.

————. "Alternative Orientations to Social Science Utilization," *Social Science Information*, IX, No. 2 (1970), 7–34.

ARGYRIS, CHRIS. "Creating Effective Relationships in Organizations," *Human Organization*, XVII, No. 1 (1958), 34–40.

ARONSON, SIDNEY H., and CLARENCE C. SHERWOOD. "Researcher Versus Practitioner: Problems in Social Action Research," *Social Work*, XII, No. 4 (1967), 89–96.

BAKER, ROBERT L. "Curriculum Evaluation," *Review of Educational Research*, XXXIX, No. 3 (1969), 339–58.

BARTON, ALLEN H. *Studying the Effects of a College Education*. New Haven, Conn.: Edward H. Hazen Foundation, 1959.

BATEMAN, WORTH. "Assessing Program Effectiveness: A Rating System for Identifying Relative Program Success," *Welfare in Review*, VI, No. 1 (1968), 1–10.

BELSHAW, CYRIL S. "Evaluation of Technical Assistance as a Contribution to Development," *International Development Review*, VIII (June 1966), 2–23.

BENEDICT, BARBARA A., PAULA H. CALDER, DANIEL M. CALLAHAN, HARVEY HORNSTEIN, and MATTHEW B. MILES. "The, Clinical-Experimental Approach to Assessing Organizational Change Efforts," *Journal of Applied Behavioral Science*, III, No. 3 (1967), 347–80.

BENNIS, WARREN. "Theory and Method in Applying Behavioral Science to Planned Organizational Change," *Journal of Applied Behavioral Science*, I, No. 4 (1965), 337–60.

———. Kenneth D. Benne, and Robert Chin, eds. *The Planning of Change* (2nd ed.). New York: Holt, Rinehart & Winston, Inc., 1969.

BERLAK, HAROLD. "Values, Goals, Public Policy and Educational Evaluation," *Review of Educational Research*, XL, No. 2 (1970), 261–78.

BERRY, DEAN. *The Politics of Personnel Research*. Ann Arbor, Mich.: Bureau of Industrial Relations, Graduate School of Business Administration, University of Michigan, 1967.

BIGMAN, STANLEY K. "Evaluating the Effectiveness of Religious Programs," *Review of Religious Research*, II, No. 3 (1961), 97–121.

BLENKNER, MARGARET. "Obstacles to Evaluative Research in Casework," *Social Casework*, XXXI, Nos. 2 and 3 (1950), Parts 1 and 2, 54–60, 97–105.

BLUM, HENDRIK L., and ALVIN R. LEONARD. "Evaluation Research and Demonstration," in *Public Administration: A Public Health Viewpoint*, pp. 286–322. New York: The Macmillan Company, 1963.

BORGATTA, EDGAR. "Research: Pure and Applied," *Group Psychotherapy*, VIII, No. 3 (1955), 263–77.

————. "Research Problems in Evaluation of Health Service Demonstrations," *Milbank Memorial Fund Quarterly,* XLIV, No. 4 (1966), Part 2, 182–99.

BRIM, ORVILLE G., JR. "Evaluating the Effects of Parent Education," *Journal of Marriage and Family Living,* XIX (February 1957), 54–60.

BROOKS, MICHAEL P. "The Community Action Program as a Setting for Applied Research," *Journal of Social Issues,* XXI, No. 1 (1965), 29–40.

BRUNNER, EDMUND DES. "Evaluation Research in Adult Education," *International Review of Community Development,* No. 17–18 (1967), 97–102.

BYNDER, HERBERT. "Sociology in a Hospital: A Case Study in Frustration," in *Sociology in Action,* ed. Arthur B. Shostak, pp. 61–70. Homewood, Ill.: Dorsey Press, 1966.

CALDWELL, MICHAEL S., "An Approach to the Assessment of Educational Planning," *Educational Technology,* VIII, No. 19 (1968), 5–12.

CAMPBELL, DONALD T. "Administrative Experimentation, Institutional Records, and Nonreactive Measures," in *Improving Experimental Design and Statistical Analysis,* ed. J. C. Stanley, pp. 257–91. Chicago: Rand McNally & Co., 1967.

————. "Reforms as Experiments," *American Psychologist,* XXIV, No. 4 (1969), 409–29.

————. "Considering the Case Against Experimental Evaluations of Social Innovations," *Administrative Science Quarterly,* XV, No. 1 (1970), 110–13.

CARO, FRANCIS G. "Approaches to Evaluative Research: A Review," *Human Organization,* XXVIII, No. 2 (1969), 87–99.

————. "Issues in the Evaluation of Social Programs," *Review of Educational Research,* XLI, No. 2 (1971), 87–114.

————, ed. *Readings in Evaluation Research.* New York: Russell Sage Foundation, 1971.

CARTER, REGINALD K. "Client's Resistance to Negative Findings and the Latent Conservative Function of Evaluation Studies," *The American Sociologist,* VI, No. 2 (1971), 118–24.

CHERNEY, PAUL R., ed. *Making Evaluation Research Useful.* Columbia, Md.: American City Corporation, 1971.

CHERNS, A. "The Use of the Social Sciences," *Human Relations,* XXI, No. 4 (1968), 313–25.

————. "Social Research and Its Diffusion," *Human Relations,* XXII, No. 3 (1969), 209–18.

COHEN, DAVID K. "Politics and Research: Evaluation of Social Action Programs in Education," *Review of Educational Research*, XL, No. 2 (1970), 213–38.

COLVIN, C. R. "A Reading Program That Failed—Or Did It?" *Journal of Reading*, XII, No. 2 (1968), 142–46.

COMMUNITY COUNCIL OF GREATER NEW YORK, RESEARCH DEPARTMENT. *Issues in Community Action Research.* Report of the Spring Research Forum on Evaluation Efforts in Three New York City Community Action Programs, 1967.

CRONBACH, LEE J. "Evaluation for Course Improvement," *Teachers College Record*, LXIV, No. 8 (1963), 672–83. Reprinted in *Readings in Measurement and Evaluation*, ed. Norman Gronlund, pp. 37–52. New York: The Macmillan Company, 1968.

DAILY, EDWIN F., and MILDRED A. MOREHEAD. "A Method of Evaluating and Improving the Quality of Medical Care," *American Journal of Public Health*, XLVI, No. 7 (1956), 848–54.

DAVIS, JAMES A. "Great Books and Small Groups: An Informal History of a National Survey," in *Sociologists at Work: Essays on the Craft of Social Research*, ed. Philip E. Hammond, pp. 212–34. New York: Basic Books, Inc., Publishers, 1964.

DENISTON, O. L., I. M. ROSENSTOCK, and V. A. GETTING. "Evaluation of Program Effectiveness," *Public Health Reports*, LXXXIII, No. 4 (1968), 323–35.

————, ————, W. WELCH, and V. A. GETTING. "Evaluation of Program Efficiency," *Public Health Reports*, LXXXIII, No. 7 (1968), 603–10.

————, and ————. "Evaluating Health Programs," *Public Health Reports*, LXXXV, No. 9 (1970), 835–40.

DEXTER, LEWIS, A. "Impressions About Utility and Wastefulness in Applied Social Science Studies," *American Behavioral Scientist*, IX, No. 6 (1966), 9–10.

DONABEDIAN, AVEDIS. "Evaluating the Quality of Medical Care," *Milbank Memorial Fund Quarterly*, XLIV, No. 3 (1966), part 2, 166–203.

DORFMAN, ROBERT. "Introduction," in *Measuring Benefits of Government Investments*, pp. 1–11. Washington, D.C.: The Brookings Institution, 1965.

DOWNS, ANTHONY. "Some Thoughts on Giving People Economic Advice," *American Behavioral Scientist*, IX, No. 1 (1965), 30–32.

DRESSEL, PAUL L., ed. *Evaluation in Higher Education.* Boston: Houghton Mifflin Company, 1961.

DREW, ELIZABETH B. "HEW Grapples with PPBS," *The Public Interest*, No. 8 (Summer 1967), 9–29.

DUBOIS, PHILIP H., and E. DOUGLAS MAYER, eds. *Research Strategies for Evaluating Training*. AERA Monograph Series on Evaluation, No. 4. Chicago: Rand McNally & Co., 1970.

DYER, HENRY S. "The Pennsylvania Plan: Evaluating the Quality of Educational Programs," *Science Education*, L, No. 3 (1966), 242–48.

EATON, JOSEPH W. "Symbolic and Substantive Evaluation Research," *Administrative Science Quarterly*, VI, No. 4 (1962), 421–42.

EDUCATIONAL EVALUATION: NEW ROLES, NEW MEANS, 68TH YEARBOOK OF THE NATIONAL SOCIETY FOR THE STUDY OF EDUCATION, ed. Ralph W. Tyler. Chicago: National Society for the Study of Education, 1969.

EDUCATIONAL TESTING SERVICE. *On Evaluating Title I Programs*. Princeton, N.J.: ETS, 1966.

EIDELL, TERRY L., and JOANNE M. KITCHEL, eds. *Knowledge Production and Utilization in Educational Administration*. Eugene, Ore.: Center for the Advanced Study of Educational Administration, University of Oregon, 1968.

ELINSON, JACK. "Effectiveness of Social Action Programs in Health and Welfare," in *Assessing the Effectiveness of Child Health Services, Report of the Fifty-sixth Ross Conference on Pediatric Research*, pp. 77–88. Columbus, O.: Ross Laboratories, 1967.

ETZIONI, AMITAI. "Two Approaches to Organizational Analysis: A Critique and a Suggestion," *Administrative Science Quarterly*, V, No. 2 (1960), 257–78.

———, and Edward W. Lehman. "Some Dangers in 'Valid' Social Measurement," *Annals of the American Academy of Political and Social Science*, Vol. 373 (September 1967), 1–15.

"EVALUATING EDUCATIONAL PROGRAMS: A SYMPOSIUM," *Urban Review*, III, No. 4 (1969), 4–22.

EVANS, JOHN W. "Evaluating Social Action Programs," *Social Science Quarterly*, L, No. 3 (1969), 568–81.

FAIRWEATHER, GEORGE W. *Methods for Experimental Social Innovation*. New York: John Wiley & Sons, Inc., 1967.

FELLIN, PHILLIP, TONY TRIPODI, and HENRY J. MEYER, eds. *Exemplars of Social Research*. Itasca, Ill.: F. E. Peacock, Publishers, Inc., 1969.

FERMAN, LOUIS A. "Some Perspectives on Evaluating Social Welfare Programs," *Annals of the American Academy of Political and Social Science*, Vol. 385 (September 1969), 143–56.

FIRST NATIONAL CONFERENCE ON EVALUATION IN PUBLIC HEALTH. Ann Arbor, Mich.: University of Michigan School of Public Health, Continued Education Series, No. 89, 1960.

FLANAGAN, JOHN C. "Evaluating Educational Outcomes," *Science Education,* L, No. 3 (1966), 248–51.

————. "Project Talent: The First National Census of Aptitudes and Abilities," in *Readings in Measurement and Evaluation,* ed. Norman Gronlund, pp. 413–21. New York: The Macmillan Company, 1968.

FLECK, ANDREW C., JR. "Evaluation as a Logical Process," *Canadian Journal of Public Health,* LII, No. 5 (1961), 185–91.

————. "Evaluation Research Programs in Public Health Practice," *Annals of the New York Academy of Sciences,* CVII, No. 2 (1963), 717–24.

FOX, DAVID J. "Issues in Evaluating Programs for Disadvantaged Children," *Urban Review,* II (December 1967), 7, 9, 11.

FREEMAN, HOWARD E., and CLARENCE C. SHERWOOD. "Research in Large-scale Intervention Programs," *Journal of Social Issues,* XXI, No. 1 (1965), 11–28.

————, and ————. *Social Research and Social Policy.* Englewood Cliffs, N.J.: Prentice-Hall, Inc., 1970.

GETTING, VLADO A. "Part II—Evaluation," *American Journal of Public Health,* XLVII, No. 4 (1957), 409–13.

GLASER, EDWARD M., and HUBERT S. COFFEY. *Utilization of Applicable Research and Demonstration Results.* Los Angeles, Calif.: Human Interaction Research Institute, 1967.

————, and HARVEY L. ROSS. *Increasing the Utilization of Applied Research Results.* Los Angeles, Calif.: Human Interaction Research Institute, 1971.

GLASS, GENE V. *The Growth of Evaluation Methodology.* AERA Monograph Series on Curriculum Evaluation, No. 7. Chicago: Rand McNally & Co., in press.

GLENNAN, THOMAS K., JR. *Evaluating Federal Manpower Programs: Notes and Observations.* Santa Monica, Calif.: The RAND Corporation, September 1969.

GLOCK, CHARLES Y. et al. *Case Studies in Bringing Behavioral Science into Use: Studies in the Utilization of Behavioral Science,* Vol. 1. Stanford, Calif.: Institute for Communication Research, 1961.

GOLLIN, ALBERT E. "The Evaluation of Overseas Programs: Applied Research and Its Organizational Context," in *Education and Training for International Living: Concepts,* ed. Robert Campbell, Bert King, and John Nagay. Arlington, Va.: Beatty Publishers, 1970.

GORHAM, WILLIAM. "Notes of a Practitioner," *The Public Interest*, No. 8 (Summer 1967), 4–8.

GREENBERG, BERNARD G., and BERWYN F. MATTISON. "The Whys and Wherefores of Program Evaluation," *Canadian Journal of Public Health*, XLVI, No. 7 (1955), 293–99.

GRIESSMAN, B. EUGENE. "An Approach to Evaluating Comprehensive Social Projects," *Educational Technology*, IX, No. 2 (1969), 16–19.

GROBMAN, HULDA. *Evaluation Activities of Curriculum Projects: A Starting Point*. AERA Monograph Series on Curriculum Evaluation, No. 2. Chicago: Rand McNally & Co., 1968.

GRUENBERG, ERNEST M., ed. "Evaluating the Effectiveness of Mental Health Services," *Milbank Memorial Fund Quarterly*, XLIV, No. 1 (1966), Part 2 (whole issue).

GUBA, EGON G. "Development, Diffusion and Evaluation," in *Knowledge Production and Utilization in Educational Administration*, ed. Terry L. Eidell and Joanne M. Kitchel, pp. 37–63. Eugene, Ore.: University Council for Educational Administration and Center for the Advanced Study of Educational Administration, University of Oregon, 1968.

————. "The Failure of Educational Evaluation," *Educational Technology*, IX, No. 5 (1969), 29–38.

————, and JOHN HORVAT. "Evaluation During Development," *Bulletin of the School of Education*. Indiana University, XLVI, No. 2 (1970), 21–45.

————, and DANIEL L. STUFFLEBEAM. "Evaluation: The Process of Stimulating, Aiding, and Abetting Insightful Action." Address delivered at Second National Symposium for Professors of Educational Research, November 21, 1968. Columbus, Ohio: Evaluation Center, College of Education, Ohio State University, 1968.

HAGEN, ELIZABETH P., and ROBERT L. THORNDIKE. "Evaluation," in *Encyclopedia of Educational Research*, 3rd ed., pp. 482–86. New York: The Macmillan Company, 1960.

HALL, RICHARD H. "The Applied Sociologist and Organizational Sociology," in *Sociology in Action*, ed. Arthur B. Shostak, pp. 33–38. Homewood, Ill.: Dorsey Press, 1966.

HARDIN, EINAR, and MICHAEL E. BORUS. "An Economic Evaluation of the Retraining Program in Michigan: Methodological Problems of Research," *Proceedings of the Social Statistics Section*. Washington, D.C.: American Statistical Association, 1966, pp. 133–37.

HASTINGS, J. THOMAS. "Curriculum Evaluation: The Why of the Outcomes," *Journal of Educational Measurement*, III, No. 3 (1966), 27–

32. Also reprinted in *Readings in Measurement and Evaluation*, ed. Norman Gronlund, pp. 53–60. New York: The Macmillan Company, 1968.

HAVELOCK, RONALD G. *Planning for Innovation Through Dissemination and Utilization of Knowledge.* Ann Arbor, Mich.: Institute for Social Research, University of Michigan, 1969.

HAYES, SAMUEL P. *Measuring the Results of Development Projects.* Paris: UNESCO, 1959.

———. *Evaluating Development Projects: A Manual for the Use of Field Workers.* Paris: UNESCO, 1966.

HEMPHILL, JOHN K. "The Relationships Between Research and Evaluation Studies," in *Educational Evaluation: New Roles, New Means, 68th Yearbook of the National Society for the Study of Education*, ed. Ralph W. Tyler, pp. 189–220. Chicago: National Society for the Study of Education, 1969.

HERMAN, MELVIN. "Problems of Evaluation," *The American Child*, XLVII, No. 2 (1965), 5–10.

———, and MICHAEL MUNK. *Decision Making in Poverty Programs: Case Studies from Youth-Work Agencies.* New York: Columbia University Press, 1968, pp. 139–81.

HERZOG, ELIZABETH. *Some Guide Lines for Evaluative Research.* Washington, D.C.: U.S. Department of Health, Education and Welfare, 1959.

HESSELING, P. "Principles of Evaluation," *Social Compass*, XI, No. 1 (1964), 5–22.

HILL, MARJORIE J., and HOWARD T. BLANE. "Evaluation of Psychotherapy with Alcoholics," *Quarterly Journal of Studies on Alcohol*, XXVIII, No. 1 (1967), 76–104.

HOLLIDAY, L. P. *Appraising Selected Manpower Training Programs in the Los Angeles Area.* Santa Monica, Calif.: The RAND Corporation, May 1969.

HOUGH, ROBBIN R. "Casualty Rates and the War on Poverty," *American Economic Review*, LVIII, No. 2 (1968), 528–32.

HOVLAND, CARL I. "Reconciling Conflicting Results Derived from Experimental and Survey Studies of Attitude Change," *American Psychologist*, XIV, No. 1 (1959), 8–17.

———, ARTHUR A. LUMSDAINE, and FRED D. SHEFFIELD. *Experiments in Mass Communication.* Princeton, N.J.: Princeton University Press, 1949.

HUTCHISON, GEORGE B. "Evaluation of Preventive Services," *Journal of Chronic Diseases*, XI, No. 5 (1960), 497–508.

HYMAN, HERBERT H., and CHARLES R. WRIGHT. "Evaluating Social Action Programs," in *The Uses of Sociology*, ed. Paul F. Lazarsfeld, William H. Sewell, and Harold L. Wilensky, pp. 741–82. New York: Basic Books, Inc., Publishers, 1967.

JAMES, GEORGE. "Research by Local Health Departments: Problems, Methods, Results," *American Journal of Public Health*, XLVIII, No. 3 (1958), 353–61.

————. "Planning and Evaluation of Health Programs," in *Administration of Community Health Services*, pp. 114–34. Chicago: International City Managers Association, 1961.

JENKS, CHARLES L. "Evaluation for a Small District," *Educational Product Report*, II, No. 5 (1967), 8–17.

JONES, JAMES A. "Research," in *Breakthrough for Disadvantaged Youth*, pp. 235–50. Washington, D.C.: U.S. Department of Labor, Manpower Administration, 1969.

JUSTMAN, JOSEPH. "Problems of Researchers in Large School Systems," *Educational Forum*, XXXII, No. 4 (1968), 429–37.

KANDEL, DENISE B., and RICHARD H. WILLIAMS. *Psychiatric Rehabilitation: Some Problems of Research*. New York: Atherton Press, Inc., 1964.

KELMAN, HOWARD R., and JACK ELINSON. "Strategy and Tactics of Evaluating a Large-scale Medical Care Program," *Proceedings of the Social Statistics Section*. Washington, D.C.: American Statistical Association, 1968, pp. 169–91.

KLINEBERG, OTTO. "The Problem of Evaluation Research," *International Social Science Bulletin*, VII, No. 3 (1955), 346–52.

KOGAN, LEONARD S., and ANN W. SHYNE. "Tender-minded and Tough-minded Approaches in Evaluative Research," *Welfare in Review*, IV, No. 2 (1966), 12–17.

KRAUSE, ELLIOTT A. "After the Rehabilitation Center," *Social Problems*, XIV, No. 2 (1966), 197–206.

LaSORTE, MICHAEL A. "The Caseworker as Research Interviewer," *The American Sociologist*, III, No. 3 (1968), 222–25.

LEMKAU, PAUL V., and BENJAMIN PASAMANICK. "Problems in Evaluation of Mental Health Programs," *American Journal of Orthopsychiatry*, XXVII, No. 1 (1957), 55–58.

LEMPERT, RICHARD. "Strategies of Research Design in the Legal Impact Study," *Law and Society Review*, I, No. 1 (1966) 111–32.

LERMAN, PAUL. "Evaluative Studies of Institutions for Delinquents: Implications for Research and Social Policy," *Social Work*, XII, No. 4 (1968), 55–64.

LEVINE, ABRAHAM S. "Evaluating Program Effectiveness and Efficiency: Rationale and Description of Research in Progress," *Welfare in Review*, V, No. 2 (1967), 1–11.

LEVINE, ROBERT A. "Evaluating the War on Poverty," in *On Fighting Poverty: Perspectives from Experience*, ed. James L. Sundquist. New York: Basic Books, Inc., Publishers, 1969, pp. 188–216.

LEVINSON, PERRY. "Evaluation of Social Welfare Programs: Two Research Models," *Welfare in Review*, IV, No. 10 (1966), 5–12.

LEVITAN, SAR. "Facts, Fancies, and Freeloaders in Evaluating Anti-Poverty Programs," *Poverty and Human Resources Abstracts*, IV, No. 6 (1969), 13–16.

LIKERT, RENSIS, and RONALD LIPPITT. "The Utilization of Social Science," in *Research Methods in the Behavioral Sciences*, ed. Leon Festinger and Daniel Katz, pp. 581–646. New York: Holt, Rinehart & Winston, Inc., 1953.

LINDVALL, C. M., and RICHARD C. COX. *Evaluation as a Tool in Curriculum Development: The IPI Evaluation Program*. AERA Monograph Series on Curriculum Evaluation, No. 5. Chicago: Rand McNally & Co., 1970.

LIPPITT, RONALD. "The Use of Social Research to Improve Social Practice," *American Journal of Orthopsychiatry*, XXXV, No. 3 (1965), 663–69.

————, JEANNE WATSON, and BRUCE WESTLEY. *The Dynamics of Planned Change*, pp. 263–72. New York: Harcourt Brace Jovanovich, Inc., 1958.

LONGOOD, ROBERT, and ARNOLD SIMMEL. "Organizational Resistance to Innovation Suggested by Research," in *Evaluating Action Programs: Readings in Social Action and Education*, ed. Carol H. Weiss. Boston: Allyn & Bacon, Inc., 1972, pp. 311–17.

LUCHTERHAND, ELMER. "Research and the Dilemmas in Developing Social Programs," in *The Uses of Sociology*, ed. Paul F. Lazarsfeld, William H. Sewell, and Harold L. Wilensky, pp. 513–17. New York: Basic Books, Inc., Publishers, 1967.

MANGUM, GARTH L. "Evaluating Manpower Programs," *Monthly Labor Review*, XCI, No. 2 (1968), 21–22.

MANN, JOHN. *Changing Human Behavior*. New York: Charles Scribner's Sons, 1965, pp. 177–214.

MANN, FLOYD, and RENSIS LIKERT. "The Need for Research on the Communication of Research Results," *Human Organization*, XI, No. 4 (1952), 15–19.

MARRIS, PETER, and MARTIN REIN. "Research," in *Dilemmas of Social Reform*, pp. 191–207. New York: Atherton Press, Inc., 1969.

MAULDIN, W. PARKER, and JOHN A. ROSS. "Family Planning Experiments: A Review of Design," *Proceedings of the Social Statistics Section*. Washington, D.C.: American Statistical Association, 1966, pp. 278–82.

McDILL, EDWARD L., MARY S. McDILL, and J. TIMOTHY SPREHE. *Strategies for Success in Compensatory Education: An Appraisal of Evaluation Research.* Baltimore, Md.: The Johns Hopkins Press, 1969.

McINTYRE, ROBERT B., and CALVIN C. NELSON. "Empirical Evaluation of Instructional Materials," *Educational Technology*, IX, No. 2 (1969), 24–27.

MERTON, ROBERT K. "Role of the Intellectual in Public Bureaucracy," in *Social Theory and Social Structure*, pp. 207–24. New York: The Free Press, 1964.

MEYER, ALAN S., and STANLEY K. BIGMAN. "Contextual Considerations in Evaluating Narcotic Addiction Control Programs," *Proceedings of the Social Statistics Section*. Washington, D.C.: American Statistical Association, 1968, pp. 175–80.

MILLER, S. M. "The Study of Man: Evaluating Action Programs," *Trans-Action*, II (March–April 1965), 38–39.

MOREHEAD, MILDRED. "The Medical Audit as an Operational Tool," *American Journal of Public Health*, LVII, No. 9 (1967), 1643–56.

MOSS, L. "The Evaluation of Fundamental Education," *International Social Science Bulletin*, VII, No. 3 (1955), 398–417.

NAGPAUL, HANS. "The Development of Social Research in an Ad Hoc Community Welfare Organization," *Journal of Human Relations*, XIV, No. 4 (1966), 620–33.

OTT, JACK M. "Classification System for Decision Situations: An Aid to Educational Planning and Evaluation," *Educational Technology*, IX, No. 2 (1969), 20–23.

OWENS, THOMAS R. "Suggested Tasks and Roles of Evaluation Specialists in Education," *Educational Technology*, VIII, No. 22 (1968), 4–10.

PARSELL, ALFRED P. "Dynamic Evaluation: The Systems Approach to Action Research." Systems Development Corporation, Santa Monica, Calif., SP-2423. Unpublished paper.

PERRY, S. E., and LYMAN WYNNE. "Role Conflict, Role Definition, and Social Change in a Clinical Research Organization," *Social Forces*, XXXVIII, No. 1 (1959), 62–65.

POPHAM, W. JAMES et al. *Instructional Objectives.* AERA Monograph Series on Curriculum Evaluation, No. 3. Chicago: Rand McNally & Co., 1969.

PROVUS, MALCOLM. "Evaluation of Ongoing Programs in the Public School System," in *Educational Evaluation: New Roles, New Means, 68th Yearbook of the National Society for the Study of Education,* ed. Ralph W. Tyler, pp. 242–83. Chicago: National Society for the Study of Education, 1969.

RIECKEN, HENRY W. "Memorandum on Program Evaluation," in *Evaluating Action Programs: Readings in Social Action and Education,* ed. Carol H. Weiss. Boston: Allyn & Bacon, Inc., 1972, pp. 85–104.

RIVLIN, ALICE M. *Systematic Thinking for Social Action.* Washington, D.C.: The Brookings Institution, 1971.

RODMAN, HYMAN, and RALPH L. KOLODNY. "Organizational Strains in the Researcher-Practitioner Relationship," in *Applied Sociology: Opportunities and Problems,* ed. Alvin Gouldner and S. M. Miller, pp. 93–113. New York: The Free Press, 1965.

ROSENBLATT, AARON. "The Practitioner's Use and Evaluation of Research," *Social Work,* XIII, No. 1 (1968), 53–59.

ROSENSHINE, BARAK. "Evaluation of Classroom Instruction," *Review of Educational Research,* XL, No. 2 (1970), 279–300.

ROSSI, PETER, H. "Boobytraps and Pitfalls in the Evaluation of Social Action Programs," *Proceedings of the Social Statistics Section.* Washington, D.C.: American Statistical Association, 1966, pp. 127–32.

————. "Evaluating Social Action Programs," *Trans-Action,* IV, No. 7 (1967), 51–53.

————. "Practice, Method, and Theory in Evaluating Social-Action Programs," in *On Fighting Poverty: Perspectives from Experience,* ed. James L. Sundquist, pp. 217–34. New York: Basic Books, Inc., Publishers, 1969.

SADOFSKY, STANLEY. "Utilization of Evaluation Results: Feedback into the Action Program," in *Learning in Action,* ed. June L. Shmelzer. Washington, D.C.: Government Printing Office, 1966, pp. 22–36.

SCANLON, R. G. "Innovation Dissemination," *Pennsylvania School Journal,* CXVI (March 1968), 375–76.

SCHULBERG, HERBERT C., and FRANK BAKER. "Program Evaluation Models and the Implementation of Research Findings," *American Journal of Public Health,* LVIII, No. 7 (1968), 1248–55.

————, ALAN SHELDON, and FRANK BAKER, eds. *Program Evaluation in the Health Fields.* New York: Behavioral Publications, Inc., 1970.

SCHWARTZ, RICHARD D. "Field Experimentation in Sociolegal Research," *Journal of Legal Education*, XIII, No. 3 (1961), 401–10.

SCRIVEN, MICHAEL. "The Methodology of Evaluation," in *Perspectives of Curriculum Evaluation*, ed. Ralph W. Tyler, Robert M. Gagné, and Michael Scriven, pp. 39–83. AERA Monograph Series on Curriculum Evaluation, No. 1. Chicago: Rand McNally & Co., 1967.

——. "An Introduction to Meta-evaluation," *Educational Product Report*, II, No. 5 (1969), 36–38.

SHELDON, ELEANOR B., and HOWARD E. FREEMAN. "Notes on Social Indicators: Promises and Potential," *Policy Sciences*, I (1970), 97–111.

SHERWOOD, CLARENCE C. "Issues in Measuring Results of Action Programs," *Welfare in Review*, V, No. 7 (1967), 13–18.

SLOCUM, W. L. "Sociological Research for Action Agencies: Some Guides and Hazards," *Rural Sociology*, XXI, No. 2 (1956), 196–99.

SMITH, BRUCE L. R. *The RAND Corporation*. Cambridge, Mass.: Harvard University Press, 1966, pp. 195–240.

SMITH, JOEL, FRANCIS M. SIM, and ROBERT C. BEALER. "Client Structure and the Research Process," in *Human Organization Research*, ed. Richard N. Adams and Jack J. Preiss, Chap. 4. Homewood, Ill.: Dorsey Press, 1960.

SOMERS, GERALD G. "Research Methodology in the Evaluation of Retraining Programmes," University of Wisconsin, Industrial Relations Research Institute Reprint Series, No, 61. Reprinted from *Labour and Automation*, Bulletin No. 1, Geneva, 1965.

STAKE, ROBERT E. "The Countenance of Educational Evaluation," *Teachers College Record*, LXVIII, No. 7 (1967), 523–40.

——. "Testing in the Evaluation of Curriculum Development," *Review of Educational Research*, XXXVIII, No. 1 (1968), 77–84.

——. "Generalizability of Program Evaluation: The Need for Limits," *Educational Product Report*, II, No. 5 (1969), 38–40.

——. "Objectives, Priorities, and Other Judgment Data," *Review of Educational Research*, XL, No. 2 (1970), 181–212.

STEIN, HERMAN D. "The Study of Organizational Effectiveness," in *Research in Social Welfare Administration*, ed. David Fanshel, pp. 22–32. New York: National Association of Social Workers, 1962.

——, GEORGE M. HOUGHAM, SERAPIO R. ZALBA. "Assessing Social Agency Effectiveness: A Goal Model," *Welfare in Review*, VI, No. 2 (1968), 13–18.

STEMBER, CHARLES H. "Evaluating Effects of an Integrated Classroom," *Urban Review*, II, No. 7 (1968), 3–4, 30–31.

STEWARD, M. A. "The Role and Function of Educational Research—I," *Educational Research*, IX, No. 1 (1966), 3–6.

STOUFFER, SAMUEL A. "Some Observations on Study Design," *American Journal of Sociology*, LV, No. 4 (1950), 355–61.

STUFFLEBEAM, DANIEL L., "The Use and Abuse of Evaluation in Title III," *Theory into Practice*, VI, No. 3 (1967), 126–33.

————. "Evaluation Under Title I of the Elementary and Secondary Education Act of 1965." Paper presented at Evaluation Conference sponsored by the Michigan State Department of Education, East Lansing, Michigan, January 1966. (ERIC EDO24-156)

————. "Evaluation as Enlightenment for Decision-Making." An address delivered at the Working Conference on Assessment Theory, sponsored by the Commission on Assessment of Education Outcomes, The Association for Supervision and Curriculum Development, Sarasota, Florida, January 19, 1968. Columbus, O.: The Evaluation Center, College of Education, The Ohio State University.

————. "Toward a Science of Educational Evaluation," *Educational Technology*, VIII, No. 14 (1968), 5–12.

STURZ, HERBERT. "Experiments in the Criminal Justice System," *Legal Aid Briefcase* (February 1967), 1–5.

SUCHMAN, EDWARD A. "A Model for Research and Evaluation on Rehabilitation," in *Sociology and Rehabilitation*, ed. Marvin B. Sussman. Washington, D.C.: American Sociological Association, 1966, pp. 52–70.

————. "Action for What? A Critique of Evaluative Research," in *The Organization, Management, and Tactics of Social Research*, ed. Richard O'Toole. Cambridge, Mass.: Schenkman Publishing Co., Inc., 1970.

————. *Evaluative Research: Principles and Practice in Public Service and Social Action Programs*. New York: Russell Sage Foundation, 1967.

TAKISHITA, JOHN Y. "Measuring the Effectiveness of a Family Planning Program: Taiwan's Experience," *Proceedings of the Social Statistics Section*. Washington, D.C.: American Statistical Association, 1966, pp. 268–71.

TAYLOR, PHILIP H. "The Role and Function of Educational Research," *Educational Research*, IX, No. 1 (1966), 11–15.

THERKILDSEN, PAUL, and PHILIP RENO. "Cost-benefit Evaluation of the Bernalillo County Work Experience Project," *Welfare in Review*, VI, No. 2 (1968), 1–12.

TRIPODI, T., I. EPSTEIN, and C. MACMURRAY. "Dilemmas in Evaluation: Implications for Administrators of Social Action Programs," *American Journal of Orthopsychiatry*, XL, No. 5 (1970), 850–57.

TURVEY, RALPH, and A. R. PREST. "Cost-benefit Analysis: A Survey," *Economic Journal*, LXXV, No. 300 (1965), 683–735.

TYLER, RALPH W. "Assessing the Progress of Education," *Science Education*, L, No. 3 (1966), 239–42.

————, ROBERT M. GAGNÉ, and MICHAEL SCRIVEN. *Perspectives of Curriculum Evaluation*. AERA Monograph Series on Curriculum Evaluation, No. 1. Chicago: Rand McNally & Co., 1967.

U.S. CONGRESS, HOUSE COMMITTEE ON GOVERNMENT OPERATIONS, RESEARCH AND TECHNICAL PROGRAMS SUBCOMMITTEE. *The Use of Social Research in Federal Domestic Programs*, Vol. III. 90th Congress, 1st session. Washington, D.C.: Government Printing Office, 1967.

U.S. DEPARTMENT OF HEALTH, EDUCATION AND WELFARE, NATIONAL ADVISORY MENTAL HEALTH COUNCIL. *Evaluation in Mental Health*. Washington, D.C.: Public Health Service, Publication No. 413, 1955.

U.S. DEPARTMENT OF HEALTH, EDUCATION AND WELFARE, OFFICE OF EDUCATION. *Preparing Evaluation Reports: A Guide for Authors*. Washington, D.C.: Government Printing Office, 1970.

WALL, W. D. "The Future of Educational Research," *Educational Research*, X, No. 3 (1968), 163–69.

WARD, DAVID A., and GENE G. KASSEBAUM. "On Biting the Hand That Feeds: Some Implications of Sociological Evaluations of Correctional Effectiveness," in *Evaluating Action Programs: Readings in Social Action and Education*, ed. Carol H. Weiss. Boston: Allyn & Bacon, Inc., 1972, pp. 300–310.

————. "Evaluations of Correctional Treatment: Some Implications of Negative Findings," in *Law Enforcement Science and Technology*, ed. S. A. Yefsky, pp. 201–9. Proceedings of the First National Symposium on Law Enforcement Science and Technology, IIT Research Institute. Washington, D.C.: Thompson Book Co., 1967.

WARDROP, JAMES L. "Generalizability of Program Evaluation: The Danger of Limits," *Educational Product Report*, II, No. 5 (1969), 41–42.

WEINBERGER, MARTIN. "Evaluating Educational Programs: Observations by a Market Researcher," *Urban Review*, III, No. 4 (1969), 23–26.

WEISS, CAROL H., ed. *Evaluating Action Programs: Readings in Social Action and Education.* Boston: Allyn & Bacon, Inc., 1972.

———. "Planning an Action Project Evaluation," in *Learning in Action,* ed. June L. Shmelzer, pp. 6–21. Washington, D.C.: Government Printing Office, 1966.

———. "Prevention of Juvenile Delinquency: Research and Evaluation," in *Papers on Research in Crime and Delinquency,* pp. 1–21. Washington, D.C.: U.S. Department of Health, Education and Welfare, Office of Juvenile Delinquency and Youth Development, December 1966.

———. "Evaluation of In-service Training," in *Targets for In-service Training,* pp. 47–54. Washington, D.C.: Joint Commission on Correctional Manpower and Training, October 1967.

———. "Utilization of Evaluation: Toward Comparative Study," in *The Use of Social Research in Federal Domestic Programs,* Vol. III, pp. 426–32. U.S. Congress, House Committee on Government Operations, Research and Technical Programs Subcommittee. 90th Congress, 1st session. Washington, D.C.: Government Printing Office, 1967.

———. "The Politicization of Evaluation Research," *Journal of Social Issues,* XXVI, No. 4 (1970), 57–68.

———. *Organizational Constraints on Evaluation Research.* New York: Bureau of Applied Social Research, 1971.

———, KAREN S. LOUIS, and JANET A. WEISS. "Abstracts of Works on Evaluation Research," in *Planning for Creative Change: Use of Program Evaluation.* Washington, D.C.: Government Printing Office, 1971.

WEISS, ROBERT S., and MARTIN REIN. "The Evaluation of Broad-aim Programs: A Cautionary Case and a Moral," *Annals of the American Academy of Political and Social Science,* Vol. 385 (September 1969), 133–42. A revised version also appears in *Administrative Science Quarterly,* XV, No. 1 (1970), 97–109.

WELCH, WAYNE W. "Curriculum Evaluation," *Review of Educational Research,* XXXIX, No. 4 (1969), 429–43.

WHOLEY, JOSEPH S. "The Absence of Program Evaluation as an Obstacle to Effective Public Expenditure Policy: A Case Study of Child Health Care Programs," in *The Analysis and Evaluation of Public Expenditures: The PPB System,* A Compendium of Papers Submitted to the Subcommittee on Economy in Government of the Joint Economic Committee, 91st Congress, 1st session, 1969, I, 451–71. Washington, D.C.: Government Printing Office, 1970.

———, et al. *Federal Evaluation Policy.* Washington, D.C.: The Urban Institute, 1970.

WILDER, DAVID E. "Problems of Evaluation Research," in *An Overview of Adult Education Research*, ed. Edmund deS. Brunner, David E. Wilder, Corinne Kirchner, and John S. Newberry, pp. 243–73. Chicago: Adult Education Association of the U.S.A., 1959.

WILKINS, LESLIE T. "Evaluation of Training Programs," in *Social Deviance*, pp. 288–93. London: Tavistock Publications, 1964.

————. *Evaluation of Penal Measures*. New York: Random House, Inc., 1969.

WILLIAMS, WALTER. "Developing an Evaluation Strategy for a Social Action Agency," *Journal of Human Resources*, IV, No. 4 (1969), 451–65.

————, and JOHN W. EVANS. "The Politics of Evaluation: The Case of Head Start," *Annals of the American Academy of Political and Social Science*, Vol. 385 (September 1969), 118–32.

WITTROCK, M. C. "The Evaluation of Instruction," *Evaluation Comment*, I, No. 4 (1969), 1–7.

WORTHEN, BLAINE R. "Toward a Taxonomy of Evaluation Designs," *Educational Technology*, VIII, No. 15 (1968), 3–9.

WRIGHT, CHARLES R., and HERBERT H. HYMAN. "The Evaluators," in *Sociologists at Work: Essays on the Craft of Social Research*, ed. Phillip E. Hammond, pp. 121–41. New York: Basic Books, Inc., Publishers, 1964.

Illustrative Evaluation Studies

ALDRICH, NELSON, ed. "The Controversy over More Effective Schools: A Special Supplement," *Urban Review*, II, No. 6 (1968), 15–34.

BENEDICT, BARBARA A., PAULA H. CALDER, DAVID M. CALLAHAN, HARVEY HORNSTEIN, and MATTHEW B. MILES. "The Clinical-Experimental Approach to Assessing Organizational Change Efforts," *Journal of Applied Behavioral Science*, III, No. 3 (1967), 347–80.

BERLEMAN, WILLIAM C., and THOMAS W. STEINBURN. "The Execution and Evaluation of a Delinquency Prevention Program," *Social Problems*, XIV, No. 4 (1967), 413–23.

BOGART, LEO et al. *Social Research and the Desegregation of the U.S. Army*. Chicago: Markham Publishing Co., 1969.

BOOCOCK, SARANE S., and JAMES S. COLEMAN. "Games with Simulated Environments in Learning," *Sociology of Education*, XXXIX, No. 3 (1966), 215–36.

CAIN, GLEN, and GERALD SOMERS. "Retraining the Disadvantaged Worker," in *Research in Vocational and Technical Education*, ed. Cathleen Quirk and Carol Sheehan, pp. 27–44. Madison, Wis.: Center for Studies in Vocational and Technical Education, University of Wisconsin, 1967.

——, and ERNST W. STROMSDORFER. "An Economic Evaluation of Government Retraining Programs in West Virginia," in *Retraining the Unemployed*, ed. Gerald Somers, pp. 299–335. Madison, Wis.: University of Wisconsin Press, 1968.

CAMPBELL, DONALD T., and H. LAURENCE ROSS. "The Connecticut Crackdown on Speeding: Time-series Data in Quasi-experimental Analysis," *Law and Society Review*, III, No. 1 (1968), 33–53.

CAPLAN, NATHAN. "Treatment Intervention and Reciprocal Interaction Effects," *Journal of Social Issues*, XXIV, No. 1 (1968), 63–88.

CHAMBERLIN, C. D., ENID CHAMBERLIN, N. E. DROUGHT, and W. E. SCOTT. *Adventure in American Education*, Vol. IV, *Did They Succeed in College?* New York: Harper and Row, Publishers, 1942.

CLARK, BURTON R. *The Open Door College: A Case Study*. New York: McGraw-Hill Book Company, 1960.

COLEMAN, JAMES S., and ERNEST Q. CAMPBELL et al. *Equality of Educational Opportunity*. Washington, D.C.: Government Printing Office, 1966.

CUMMING, ELAINE, and JOHN CUMMING. *Closed Ranks: Study of Mental Health Education*. Cambridge, Mass.: Harvard University Press, 1957.

DAVIS, JAMES A. *Great Books and Small Groups*. New York: The Free Press, 1961.

DENTLER, ROBERT. *The Young Volunteers: An Evaluation of Three Programs of the American Friends Service Committee*. Chicago: National Opinion Research Center, 1959.

DRESSEL, PAUL L. *Evaluation in General Education*. Dubuque, Iowa: William C. Brown Company, Publishers, 1954.

EYSENCK, H. J. "The Effects of Psychotherapy: An Evaluation," *Journal of Consulting Psychology*, XVI (1952), 319–24.

FAIRWEATHER, GEORGE W. *Social Psychology in Treating Mental Illness*. New York: John Wiley & Sons, Inc., 1964.

GOLLIN, ALBERT E. *Education for National Development: Effects of U.S. Technical Training Programs*. New York: Praeger Publishers, Inc., 1969.

GRANGER, R. L. et al. *The Impact of Head Start: An Evaluation of the Effects of Head Start on Children's Cognitive and Affective Develop-*

ment, Vol. I. Report to the Office of Economic Opportunity by Westinghouse Learning Corporation and Ohio University, June 1969.

GREELEY, ANDREW M., and PETER H. ROSSI. *The Education of Catholic Americans*. Chicago: Aldine-Atherton, Inc., 1966.

HAMMOND, K. R., and F. KERN. *Teaching Comprehensive Medical Care*. Cambridge, Mass.: Harvard University Press, 1959.

HYMAN, HERBERT H., CHARLES R. WRIGHT, and TERENCE K. HOPKINS. *Applications of Methods of Evaluation: Four Studies of the Encampment for Citizenship*. Los Angeles, Calif.: University of California Press, 1962.

JACOB, PHILIP E. *Changing Values in College*. New York: Harper and Row, Publishers, 1957.

KASSEBAUM, GENE, DAVID WARD, and DANIEL WILNER. *Prison Treatment and Parole Survival: An Empirical Assessment*. New York: John Wiley & Sons, Inc., 1971.

KATZ, IRWIN. "Review of Evidence on Effects of Desegregation on the Intellectual Performance of Negroes," *American Psychologist*, XIX, No. 6 (1964), 381–99.

KELLNER, ROBERT. "The Evidence in Favour of Psychotherapy," *British Journal of Medical Psychology*, XL, No. 4 (1967), 341–58.

KELMAN, H. R. "An Experiment in the Rehabilitation of Nursing Home Patients," *Public Health Reports*, No. 77 (April 1962), 356–66.

KENDALL, PATRICIA. "Evaluating an Experimental Program in Medical Education," in *Innovations in Education*, ed. Matthew B. Miles, pp. 343–60. New York: Teachers College, Bureau of Publications, 1964.

LANDERS, JACOB. *Higher Horizons: Progress Report*. New York: Board of Education of the City of New York, January 1963.

LIPTON, DOUGLAS, ROBERT MARTINSON, and JUDITH WILKS. *Treatment Evaluation Survey*. Albany, N.Y.: Office of Crime Control Planning, State of New York, 1971.

MAIN, EARL D. "A Nationwide Evaluation of M.D.T.A. Institutional Job Training," *Journal of Human Resources*, III, No. 2 (1968), 159–70.

McCORD, WILLIAM, and JOAN McCORD. *Origins of Crime: A New Evaluation of the Cambridge-Somerville Youth Study*. New York: Columbia University Press, 1959.

McDILL, EDWARD L., MARY S. McDILL, and J. TIMOTHY SPREHE. *Strategies for Success in Compensatory Education: An Appraisal of Evaluation Research*. Baltimore, Md.: The Johns Hopkins Press, 1969.

MEYER, H. J., and E. F. BORGATTA. *An Experiment in Mental Patient Rehabilitation*. New York: Russell Sage Foundation, 1959.

————, ————, and W. C. JONES. *Girls at Vocational High.* New York: Russell Sage Foundation, 1965.

MILES, MATTHEW. "Changes During and Following Laboratory Training: A Clinical-Experimental Study," *Journal of Applied Behavioral Science,* I, No. 3 (1965), 215–42.

MILLER, WALTER B. "The Impact of a 'Total-Community' Delinquency Control Project," *Social Problems,* X, No. 2 (1962), 168–91.

NEWCOMB, THEODORE M. *Personality and Social Change.* New York: The Dryden Press, 1957.

OFFICE OF ECONOMIC OPPORTUNITY. *Preliminary Results of the New Jersey Graduated Work Incentive Experiment.* Washington, D.C.: OEO, 1970.

————. *Further Preliminary Results of the New Jersey Graduated Work Incentive Experiment.* Washington, D.C.: OEO, 1971.

————. *Reports from the 100-City CAP Evaluation.* Washington, D.C.: OEO, 1970.

PATTISON, E. MANSELL, RONALD COE, and ROBERT J. RHODES. "Evaluation of Alcoholism Treatment: A Comparison of Three Facilities," *Archives of General Psychiatry,* XX, No. 4 (1969), 478–88.

POPHAM, W. J., and J. M. SADNAVITCH. "Filmed Science Courses in the Public School: An Experimental Approach," *Science Education,* XLV, No. 4 (1961), 327–35.

POWERS, EDWIN, and HELEN WITMER. *An Experiment in the Prevention of Juvenile Delinquency: The Cambridge-Somerville Youth Study.* New York: Columbia University Press, 1951.

PRICE, BRONSON. *School Health Services: A Selective Review of Evaluative Studies.* Washington, D.C.: U.S. Department of Health, Education and Welfare, Social Security Administration, Children's Bureau, 1957.

RIECKEN, HENRY. *The Volunteer Work Camp: A Psychological Evaluation.* Reading, Mass.: Addison-Wesley Publishing Co., Inc., 1952.

ROGERS, CARL R., and ROSALIND F. DYMOND. *Psychotherapy and Personality Change.* Chicago: University of Chicago Press, 1954.

ROSENTHAL, ROBERT, and LENORE JACOBSON. *Pygmalion in the Classroom.* New York: Holt, Rinehart & Winston, Inc., 1968.

ROSS, H. LAURENCE, DONALD T. CAMPBELL, and GENE V. GLASS. "Determining the Social Effects of a Legal Reform: The British 'Breathalyser' Crackdown of 1967," *American Behavioral Scientist,* XIII, No. 4 (1970), 493–509.

SHELDON, ALAN. "An Evaluation of Psychiatric After-care," *British Journal of Psychiatry*, CX (1964), 662–67.

SILVER, G. *Family Medical Care*. Cambridge, Mass.: Harvard University Press, 1963.

SMITH, E. R., and R. W. TYLER. *Appraising and Recording Student Progress*. New York: Harper and Row, Publishers, 1942.

SOMERS, GERALD G. "Evaluation of Work Experience and Training of Older Workers." Madison, Wis.: Industrial Relations Research Institute, University of Wisconsin, 1967. (S)

STROMSDORFER, ERNST W. "Determinants of Economic Success in Retraining the Unemployed: The West Virginia Experience," *Journal of Human Resources*, III, No. 2 (1968), 139–52.

THOMSON, CAPTANE P., and NORMAN W. BELL. "Evaluation of a Rural Community Mental Health Program," *Archives of General Psychiatry*, XX, No. 4 (1969), 448–56.

U.S. DEPARTMENT OF AGRICULTURE, Agricultural Marketing Service, Food Distribution Division. *The Food Stamp Program: An Initial Evaluation of the Pilot Project*. Washington, D.C.: Government Printing Office, April 1962.

U.S. DEPARTMENT OF HEALTH, EDUCATION AND WELFARE, National Advisory Mental Health Council. *Evaluation in Mental Health*. Washington, D.C.: Public Health Service Publication No. 413, 1955.

———. *A Bibliographic Index of Evaluation in Mental Health*, prepared by James K. Dent. Washington, D.C.: Public Health Service Publication No. 1545, October 1966.

VANECKO, JAMES J. "Community Mobilization and Institutional Change," *Social Science Quarterly*, L, No. 3 (1969), 609–30.

———, with the assistance of SUSAN R. ORDEN, and SIDNEY HOLLANDER. *Community Organization Efforts, Political and Institutional Change, and the Diffusion of Change Produced by Community Action Programs*, NORC Report No. 122. Chicago: National Opinion Research Center, University of Chicago, April 1970.

WALLACE, D. *The Chemung County Research Demonstration with Dependent Multi-problem Families*. New York: State Charities Aid Association, 1965.

WALLEN, NORMAN E., and ROBERT M. W. TRAVERS. "Analysis and Investigation of Teaching Methods," in *Handbook of Research on Teaching*, ed. N. L. Gage, Chap. 10. Chicago: Rand McNally & Co., 1963.

WEEKS, H. ASHLEY. *Youthful Offenders at Highfields.* Ann Arbor, Mich.: The University of Michigan Press, 1958.

WEISBROD, BURTON A. "Preventing High School Dropouts," in *Measuring Benefits of Government Investments,* ed. Robert Dorfman. Washington, D.C.: The Brookings Institution, 1965.

WILNER, DANIEL M., R. P. WALKLEY, T. C. PINKERTON, and M. TAYBACK. *The Housing Environment and Family Life.* Baltimore, Md.: The Johns Hopkins Press, 1962.

WRIGHTSTONE, J. WAYNE, SAMUEL D. McCLELLAND, JUDITH I. KRUGMAN, HERBERT HOFFMAN, NORMAN TIEMAN, and LINDA YOUNG. *Assessment of the Demonstration Guidance Project.* New York: Board of Education of the City of New York, Division of Research and Evaluation, n.d.

References on Design, Measurement, Sampling, and Analysis

ADAMS, GEORGIA S. *Measurement and Evaluation in Education, Psychology, and Guidance.* New York: Holt, Rinehart & Winston, Inc., 1964.

ANASTASI, ANNE. *Psychological Testing* (3rd ed.). New York: The Macmillan Company, 1968.

BARTON, ALLEN H. *Organizational Measurement.* Princeton, N.J.: College Entrance Examination Board, 1961.

————. "Measuring the Values of Individuals," *Religious Education,* Supplement (July–August 1962), 62–97.

BLALOCK, HUBERT M., JR., *Causal Inferences in Nonexperimental Research,* Chapel Hill, N.C.: University of North Carolina Press, 1961.

————. *An Introduction to Social Research.* Englewood Cliffs, N.J.: Prentice-Hall, Inc., 1970.

————. *Theory Construction.* Englewood Cliffs, N.J.: Prentice-Hall, Inc., 1969.

BLOOM, BENJAMIN S. et al. *Taxonomy of Educational Objectives. Handbook I: Cognitive Domain.* New York: David McKay Co., Inc., 1956.

BONJEAN, CHARLES M., RICHARD J. HILL, and S. DALE McLEMORE. *Sociological Measurement: An Inventory of Scales and Indices.* San Francisco, Calif.: Chandler Publishing Co., 1967.

BORUS, MICHAEL E., and WILLIAM R. TASH. *Measuring the Impact of Manpower Programs: A Primer,* Policy Papers in Human Resources and Industrial Relations, No. 17. Ann Arbor, Mich.: Institute of Labor and Industrial Relations, 1970.

BUROS, OSCAR, ed. *Personality Tests and Reviews.* Highland Park, N.J.: Gryphon Press, 1970.

————. *Sixth Mental Measurements Yearbook.* Highland Park, N.J.: Gryphon Press, 1965.

CAMPBELL, DONALD T., and ALBERT ERLEBACHER. "How Regression Artifacts in Quasi-Experimental Evaluations Can Mistakenly Make Compensatory Education Look Harmful," in *Compensatory Education: A National Debate,* Vol. 3 of *The Disadvantaged Child,* ed. J. Hellmuth. New York: Brunner/Mazel, Inc., 1970.

————, and DONALD W. FISKE. "Convergent and Discriminant Validation by the Multitrait-Multimethod Matrix," *Psychological Bulletin,* LVI, No. 2 (1959), 81–105.

————, and JULIAN STANLEY. "Experimental and Quasi-Experimental Designs for Research on Teaching," in *Handbook of Research on Teaching,* ed. N. L. Gage, pp. 171–246. Chicago: Rand McNally & Co., 1963. Reprinted as *Experimental and Quasi-Experimental Designs for Research.* Chicago: Rand McNally & Co., 1966.

COCHRAN, WILLIAM G. *Sampling Techniques.* New York: John Wiley & Sons, Inc., 1953.

COX, DAVID R. *Planning of Experiments.* New York: John Wiley & Sons, Inc., 1958.

CRONBACH, LEE J. *Essentials of Psychological Testing* (3rd ed.). New York: Harper & Row, Publishers, 1970.

DAVIS, JAMES A. *Elementary Survey Analysis.* Englewood Cliffs, N.J.: Prentice-Hall, Inc., 1971.

DUNCAN, OTIS DUDLEY. "Path Analysis: Sociological Examples," *American Journal of Sociology,* LXXII, No. 1 (1966), 1–16.

FESTINGER, LEON, and D. KATZ. *Research Methods in the Behavioral Sciences.* New York: Holt, Rinehart & Winston, Inc., 1953.

GAGE, N. L., ed. *Handbook of Research on Teaching.* Chicago: Rand McNally & Co., 1963.

GRONLUND, NORMAN, ed. *Readings in Measurement and Evaluation.* New York: The Macmillan Company, 1968.

GROUP FOR THE ADVANCEMENT OF PSYCHIATRY, *Psychiatric Research and the Assessment of Change,* Vol. 6, Report No. 63, New York, 1966.

HANSEN, MORRIS H., WILLIAM N. HURWITZ, and WILLIAM G. MADOW. *Sample Survey Methods and Theory,* Vol 1: *Method and Applications.* New York: John Wiley & Sons, Inc., 1953.

HARRIS, CHESTER W., ed. *Problems in Measuring Change.* Madison, Wis.: University of Wisconsin Press, 1963.

HAYS, W. L. *Statistics for Psychologists.* New York: Holt, Rinehart & Winston, Inc., 1963.

HOCHSTIM, JOSEPH R. "A Critical Comparison of Three Strategies of Collecting Data from Households," *Journal of the American Statistical Association,* LXII, No. 319 (1967), 976–89.

HYMAN, HERBERT. *Survey Design and Analysis: Principles, Cases, and Procedures.* New York: The Free Press, 1955.

KAHN, ROBERT L., and CHARLES F. CANNELL. *The Dynamics of Interviewing.* New York: John Wiley & Sons, Inc., 1957.

KAPLAN, ABRAHAM. *The Conduct of Inquiry.* Scranton, Pa.: Chandler Publishing Co., 1964.

KENDALL, PATRICIA L. "A Review of Indicators Used in 'The American Soldier,' " in *The Language of Social Research,* ed. Paul F. Lazarsfeld and Morris Rosenberg, pp. 37–39. New York: The Free Press, 1955.

KIRK, ROGER E. *Experimental Design: Procedures for the Behavioral Sciences.* Belmont, Calif.: Brooks/Cole Publishing Co., 1968.

KISH, LESLIE. "Selection of the Sample," in *Research Methods in the Behavioral Sciences,* ed. Leon Festinger and Daniel Katz, pp. 175–239. New York: The Dryden Press, 1953.

———. *Survey Sampling.* New York: John Wiley & Sons, Inc., 1965.

KRATHWOHL, DAVID R., BENJAMIN S. BLOOM, and BERTRAN B. MASIA. *Taxonomy of Educational Objectives. Handbook II: Affective Domain.* New York: David McKay Co., Inc., 1964.

LINDZEY, GARDNER, and ELLIOT ARONSON, eds. *The Handbook of Social Psychology* (2nd ed.). Vol. II, *Research Methods.* Reading, Mass.: Addison-Wesley Publishing Co. Inc., 1968.

MICHAEL, WILLIAM G., and NEWTON S. METFESSEL. "A Paradigm for Developing Valid Measurable Objectives in the Evaluation of Educational Programs in Colleges and Universities," *Educational and Psychological Measurement,* XXVII, No. 2 (1967), 373–83.

MILLER, DELBERT C. *Handbook of Research Design and Social Measurement.* New York: David McKay Co., Inc., 1964.

MONROE, J., and A. L. FINKNER. *Handbook of Area Sampling.* Philadelphia: Chilton Book Company, 1959.

OPPENHEIM, A. N. *Questionnaire Design and Attitude Measurement.* New York: Basic Books, Inc., Publishers, 1966.

PLUTCHIK, R., S. R. PLATMAN, and R. R. FIEVE. "Three Alternatives to the Double-Blind," *Archives of General Psychiatry*, XX (1969), 428–32.

ROBINSON, J. P., R. ATHANASIOU, and KENDRA B. HEAD. *Measures of Occupational Attitudes and Occupational Characteristics*. Ann Arbor, Mich.: Survey Research Center, University of Michigan, 1967.

————, JERROLD G. RUSK, and KENDRA B. HEAD. *Measures of Political Attitudes*. Ann Arbor, Mich.: Survey Research Center, University of Michigan, 1968.

————, and PHILLIP R. SHAVER. *Measures of Social Psychological Attitudes*. Ann Arbor, Mich.: Survey Research Center, University of Michigan, 1969.

ROSENBERG, MORRIS. *The Logic of Survey Analysis*. New York: Basic Books, Inc., Publishers, 1968.

RUSSETT, B. M. et al. *World Handbook of Political and Social Indicators*. New Haven, Conn. and London: Yale University Press, 1964.

SHAW, MARVIN E., and JACK M. WRIGHT. *Scales for the Measurement of Attitudes*. New York: McGraw-Hill Book Company, 1967.

SJOBERG, GIDEON, and ROGER NETT. *A Methodology for Social Research*. New York: Harper & Row, Publishers, 1968.

SJOGREN, DOUGLAS D. "Measurement Techniques in Evaluation," *Review of Educational Research*, XL, No. 2 (1970), 301–20.

SLONIM, MORRIS JAMES. *Sampling*. New York: Simon & Schuster, Inc., 1966.

STEPHAN, FREDERICK F., and PHILIP J. McCARTHY. *Sampling Opinions; An Analysis of Survey Procedure*. New York: John Wiley & Sons, Inc., 1958.

SUDMAN, SEYMOUR. *Reducing the Cost of Surveys*. Chicago: Aldine-Atherton, Inc., 1967.

THORNDIKE, ROBERT L., and ELIZABETH HAGEN. *Measurement and Evaluation in Psychology and Education* (2nd ed.). New York: John Wiley & Sons, 1961.

UNDERHILL, RALPH. "Methods in the Evaluation of Programs for Poor Youth." Chicago: National Opinion Research Center, June 1968.

U.S. BUREAU OF THE BUDGET, Executive Office of the President, *Household Survey Manual, 1969*. Available from Clearinghouse for Federal Scientific and Technical Information, Springfield, Virginia 22151, Document No. PB 18 7444.

WALKER, HELEN M., and JOSEPH LEV. *Statistical Inference*. New York: Holt, Rinehart & Winston, Inc., 1953.

WEBB, E. J., D. T. CAMPBELL, R. D. SCHWARTZ, and L. B. SE-

CHREST. *Unobtrusive Measures: Nonreactive Research in the Social Sciences.* Chicago: Rand McNally & Co., 1966.

WINER, B. J. *Statistical Principles in Experimental Design.* New York: McGraw-Hill Book Company, 1962.

ZEISEL, HANS. "Reducing the Hazards of Human Experiments through Modifications in Research Design," *Annals of the New York Academy of Sciences,* Vol. 169 (1970), 475–86.

Index

155

Managers of programs (*see* Administrators of programs)
Mann, Floyd, 113*n*
Mann, John, 48*n*, 95
McCord, Joan, 39*n*
McCord, William, 39*n*
McDill, Edward L., 41*n*, 64*n*, 98*n*
McDill, Mary S., 41*n*, 56*n*, 64*n*, 98*n*
McIntyre, Robert B., 41*n*
McLemore, S. Dale, 35
Measurement (*see also* Measures):
  of outcomes, 34–42
  of program goals, 26–27
Measures:
  development, 34–36
  handbooks, 35
  of individual change, 39–41
  of input variables, 45–47
  of institutional change, 41–42
  of intervening variables, 47–53
  of larger systems, 42
  multiple, 36–37
  proximate, 37–39
  of public attitudes, 42
  unobtrusive, 54
  validity and reliability, 36
  views of practitioners, 100–101
Merton, Robert K., 21*n*
Meyer, Alan S., 108
Meyer, H. J., 39*n*, 63*n*
Middleman in research utilization, 112, 120–21
Miller, Delbert C., 35
Miller, Ernest G., 89*n*
Miller, Walter B., 39*n*
Models:
  goal, for evaluation, 29–30
  dynamic, need for, 94
  path analysis, 51
  program process, 50–53, 75
  system, for evaluation, 29–30
More Effective Schools program, 115*n*
Morehead, Mildred, 41*n*
Morgan, James N., 51*n*
Moynihan, Daniel P., 128

Nader, Ralph, 120*n*
Nagpaul, Hans, 107*n*
Negative findings, 126–28
Nelson, Calvin C., 41*n*
Nonequivalent control groups:
  in nonexperimental design, 76–77
  in quasi-experimental design, 69–72
  regression effects, 70–71
  self-selection, 70–72, 76
  use of matching, 69–70

Nonexperimental design, 73–77
  after-only, 75–76
  with comparison groups, 76–77
  characteristics, 73–74
  one-project before-and-after, 75

Observation:
  of program, 44–45
  of outcomes, 54
Orden, Susan R., 81*n*
Organizations:
  characteristics that affect evaluator-practitioner relationships, 101–2
  effect on program, 107–9
  effects of program on, 41–42
  remedies for resistance to evaluation results, 116–21
  resistance to change, 3
  resistance to utilization of evaluation results, 113–15
  structure for evaluation, 21–23
Outcomes:
  measures of, 34–42
  types of, 39–42
  valued by practitioners, 100–101
"Outside" evaluation, 19–21

Parsell, Alfred P., 94*n*
Path analysis, 51*n*
Performance contracting, 118
Planned change, 117–18
Planning-Programming-Budgeting system (PPBS), 88–91, 121
Policy makers:
  expectations from evaluation, 14
  in similar organizations, 121–24
  types of decisions faced, 22–23
  users of evaluation, 18, 119, 121–22, 124
  when responsible for evaluation, 21–23
Powers, Edwin, 39*n*
Practitioners:
  expectations from evaluation, 14
  involvement in evaluation, 105
  lack of clarity of goals, 27
  objections to experiments, 63, 103
  relationships with evaluators, 7, 98–107
  users of evaluation, 18
Privacy, 56
Program:
  characteristics, 4–5
  clients (*see* Program participants)
  complexities, 25
  context, 107–9
  failure, 38–39, 127–28